DATE			

BREAD—AND ROSES

The Library of American History
General editor: John Anthony Scott

BREAD—AND ROSES

THE STRUGGLE OF AMERICAN LABOR
1865–1915

Milton Meltzer

Illustrated with contemporary
prints & photographs

Facts On File

New York • Oxford • Sydney

Bread—and Roses: The Struggle of American Labor, 1865–1915
Copyright © 1991 by Milton Meltzer

Originally published in a different form by Alfred A. Knopf, Inc., © 1967

Facts On File, Inc.
460 Park Avenue South
New York NY 10016
USA

Facts On File Limited
Collins Street
Oxford OX4 1XJ
United Kingdom

Library of Congress Cataloging-in-Publication Data

Meltzer. Milton, 1915-
Bread—and roses: the struggle of American labor, 1865–1915 /
Milton Meltzer.

p. cm. — (The Library of American history)
Includes bibliographical references and index.

Summary: Uses original source material to portray the momentous changes that took place in American labor, industry, and trade-unionism following the Civil War. Focuses on the work environment
in this early age of mass production and mechanization, and shows
how abusive conditions often led to labor unrest.

ISBN 0-8160-2371-9
1. Labor movement—United States—History. 2. Trade-unions—
United States—History. 3. United States—Social conditions—1865–1918.
4. II fa04 06-14-90.] I. Title. II. Series.
HD8072.M328   1991
331.88'0973—dc20   90-39759

A British CIP catalogue record for this book is available from the British Library.

Text design by Donna Sinisgalli
Jacket design by Solonay/Mitchell Associates
Composition by Facts On File, Inc.
Manufactured by the Maple-Vail Book Manufacturing Group
Printed in the United States of America

10 9 8 7 6 5 4 3 2 1

This book is printed on acid-free paper.

CONTENTS

Preface   vii

1 Revolution by Machine   1
2 Only Bread, and Nothing More?   4
3 Women Who Work   12
4 Children in the Mills   18
5 Tenements and Sweatshops   26
6 Who Owns America?   34
7 Bread or Blood   44
8 I Love This Union Cause   50
9 Rebellion on the Railroads   57
10 Dream—and Reality   66
11 A Bomb at Haymarket   76
12 Which Way: Gompers or Debs?   87
13 The Battle of Homestead   94
14 A Model Town Goes on Strike   103
15 Reformers and Radicals   112
16 Bread—and Roses Too!   119
17 Massacre at Ludlow   134
18 Conclusion   150

A Short Dictionary of Labor Terms   153
Bibliography   158
Index   164

PREFACE

Millions of American young people passing through our schools and colleges learn their United States history almost exclusively from standard textbooks. Growing dissatisfaction with these texts was eloquently voiced when Frances Fitzgerald published *America Revised: History Schoolbooks in the Twentieth Century* in 1979. High school history texts, Fitzgerald charged, are supremely dull and uninteresting. They fail to hold the attention of young people or to fire their imagination. United States history ought to arouse wonder, compassion and delight, but these books turn it into a crashing bore. One of the reasons for this, she said, is that often the texts do not draw upon the marvelous original sources that this nation inherits, which constitute the lifeblood of history, and which are indispensable to its study, no matter what the age of the student.

Efforts to find alternatives to the traditional texts began some years before Fitzgerald's book appeared. One of these was an initiative that Alfred A. Knopf launched in 1966. The result was the publication, during the years 1967–77, of an historical series designed for the use of high school students and of undergraduates and entitled The Living History Library. In all, fifteen volumes were published in this series. Each book was written by a distinguished historian or teacher. Each told the story of a different period or topic in American history—the colonial period, the American Revolution, black participation in the Civil War, the cowboy in the West, the Great Depression, and so on. Each was based on original sources, woven throughout into the framework of the narrative. Ordinary people who witnessed historical events and participated in historical struggles provided their own testimony and told their own story both in word and song. The series presented the American experience through the medium of a new literary art form. People long dead and struggles long past came to life again in the present.

The historical and literary value of these books has not diminished with the passage of time. On the contrary, the need for books such as these is greater today than it has ever been before. Innumerable important topics in our history await treatment of this type. Facts On File is happy to publish new and updated editions of the Living History Library books as part of its Library of American History.

Bread—and Roses tells the story of American working people in the fifty years between the Civil War and World War I. In those years millions of men, women and children left their villages and farms in the Old World and the New and went to toil in the cities and the factories of America's rising industrial empire. Workers and eyewitnesses tell what life was like in the mines, mills and sweatshops where people were obliged to work and in the company towns, tenements and shacks where they were obliged to live. We learn how the workers organized into unions and how they battled and suffered in the great strikes and slumps that shook the nation. This was an epic of struggle for human freedom and for a better life that gave expression to an imperishable democratic tradition in America.

John Anthony Scott

1

REVOLUTION BY MACHINE

When the cannon roared at Sumter in 1861, hundreds of thousands of young workers left the factories and took up arms. The first company mobilized to march to Washington's defense were volunteers from Lowell's textile mills. Before the last gun was silenced at Appomattox, over half of America's workingmen had stood on bloody ground.

The war that freed the slaves transformed the nation's industrial life. More than a million dollars a day were spent on weapons, ammunition, machinery, clothing, boots, shoes, canned goods. Old factories were remade and giant new ones sprang up, using faster, better methods of manufacture. Thousands of miles of railroads and telegraph wires laced the country together.

The returned soldiers became an army of volunteers in the industrial revolution. They swept over the prairies and mountains, digging out the iron ore, the coal and the oil, the silver and the gold. They manned the machines of countless new industries.

It was a revolution whose seeds had been planted a generation earlier. Even before the war the merchants of the big Atlantic seaports had backed railroad construction to reach the markets of the Ohio valley. Cheap, rapid transportation knitted town and country together. As the railroads tracked across the land, they used up more and more iron and steel. To meet the demand, new foundries and blast furnaces belched their smoke and flame over the green fields. The swiftly expanding iron and steel industry, spurred on by the railroads, became the foundation on which industrial America soared.

By opening up every corner of the country, the railroads changed the whole nature of the businessman's market, bringing vast new markets within his reach. He was spurred on to develop new ways of producing in large quantities, thereby saving costs and increasing profits. Mass production methods were introduced everywhere they could apply—in iron and steel, in textiles and shoes, in lumbering, meat packing, flour milling.

The heart of the change lay in standardizing parts and processes. It was a method of manufacture first developed by Eli Whitney in the making of guns. You made a standard item, and made it exactly the same way every time. You used exact measurements, so that any part could be replaced by an identical part.

Mass production left no place for the individual craftsman—the tailor who made the whole suit, the shoemaker who made the whole shoe, the mechanic who made the whole machine. The jacks-of all-trades, such as the village blacksmith, long the pride of his community, began to disappear. In his place you had many workers dependent upon one another to make *one* product, each swiftly trained to do a narrow part of the job.

Everything was changing for the postwar worker. Born into a nation of farmers, independent craftsmen and small manufacturers, living largely on the countryside, he or she came of age in a nation of great capitalists and big factories, massing wage earners in the cities.

Take Paterson, New Jersey. Before the Civil War, nearby New Yorkers enjoyed riding over to the upcountry hamlet to see its fine waterfall. In just one generation the rural folk of Paterson saw a city they hardly recognized spring up around them. The four silk mills that employed 590 workers before the war had now exploded into 14 mills employing 8,000 workers. The one machine shop that boasted 10 workers now had 1,100. Paterson itself had swollen from 11,000 inhabitants to 33,000.

The "up-country hamlet" was now a major industrial city. It led the country in silk textile production, exported huge quantities of mosquito netting to Africa and Asia, made one out of every four of the nation's locomotives, and made much of the ironwork used in New York's and Pennsylvania's big new buildings and bridges.

Multiply Paterson by a thousand towns and you can see what was happening. From the Civil War to 1900 the nation's population and the value of its farm products would triple. But the value of the products flooding out of the factories would increase *eleven* times.

Looking at it from the outside, it was a great victory for the human race, whose labor and inventiveness had created machines to conquer the forces of nature. What would the new industrial system mean for workers and their families? What changes would it make in their lives? How would it benefit them? What would it cost?

2

ONLY BREAD, AND NOTHING MORE?

As industry became bigger and more mechanized, thousands of skilled craftsmen saw the nature of their work change. In 1883 a young mechanic described to a United States Senate committee the shifts taking place in his trade:

> The trade has been subdivided and those subdivisions have been again subdivided, so that a man never learns the machinist's trade now. Ten years ago he learned, not the whole trade, but a fair portion of it. Also, there is more machinery used in the business, which again makes machinery . . . It is merely laborers' work . . .
>
> One man may make just a particular part of a machine and may not know anything whatever about another part of the same machine. In that way machinery is produced a great deal cheaper than it used to be formerly, and in fact, through this system of work, 100 men are able to do now what it took 300 or 400 men to do fifteen years ago . . . They so simplify the work that it is made a great deal easier and put together a great deal faster. There is no system of apprenticeship, I may say, in the business. You simply go in and learn whatever branch you are put at, and you stay at that unless you are changed to another.

Did such specialized work have any effect on a man's thinking?

It has a very demoralizing effect upon the mind throughout. The man thinks of nothing else but that particular branch; he knows that he cannot leave that particular branch and go to any other; he has got no chance whatever to learn anything else because he is kept steadily and constantly at that particular thing.

Could a man working in a machine shop hope to rise, to become a boss or a manufacturer himself?

There is no chance. They have lost all desire to become bosses now . . . because the trade has become demoralized. First they earn so small wages; and, next, it takes so much capital to become a boss now that they cannot think of it, because it takes all they can earn to live.

One immigrant from England wrote back to his friends in Sheffield:

They do far more with machinery in all trades than you do. Men never learn to do a knife through, as they do in Sheffield. The knives go through forty or fifty hands.

Shoemakers, tailors, dyers, tanners arriving hopefully from abroad found work in the United States quite unlike what they knew back home. It was chiefly workers in the building trades who found their craft was not being replaced by machinery. The machine was slow to enter mining and railway construction, too. But in iron, steel and textiles change was very rapid.

Skilled puddlers and broilers saw their jobs disappear when Bessemer and open-hearth furnaces took over production of steel ingots. The output of Bessemer ingots jumped nine times between 1874 and 1882. In the cotton and wool industries, too, a new technique called ring-spinning replaced mule-spinning, a highly skilled occupation. One mill superintendent told a reporter this story:

The mule-spinners are a tough crowd to deal with. A few years ago they were giving trouble at this mill, so one Saturday afternoon, after they had gone home, we started right in and smashed up a room-full of mules with sledgehammers. When the men came back on Monday morning, they were astonished to find that there was no work for them. That room is now full of ring frames run by girls.

The shoe industry was the classic example of what was happening. Pressed by Civil War demands for huge quantities of shoes, the mill owners introduced automatic machinery. Asked by a Congressional committee in 1899 to describe changes in work and wages in his trade, a leader of the Boot and Shoe Workers' Union said:

Eleven years ago I used to be able to earn myself, lasting shoes, from $18 to $35 in a week, according to how hard I wanted to work; that is, in the city of Lynn. Today, on the same class of work, I would not be able, on any job in the city, to make over $15, and probably my wage would run near $12 . . . And another thing; where a man at that time would likely get eight or nine months' good work in a year, at the present time the season is shorter . . . The manufacturers equip themselves to turn out their product in a shorter time, and the seasons of employment are shorter and more uncertain.

With about 100 subdivisions of labor in the making of a shoe, the worker became specialized in one simple operation. Asked what effect that had upon him, Mr. Eaton replied:

He becomes a mere machine . . . Take the proposition of a man operating a machine to nail on 40 to 60 cases of heels in a day. That is 2,400 pairs, 4,800 shoes, in a day. One not accustomed to it would wonder how a man could pick up and lay down 4,800 shoes in a day; to say nothing of putting them on a jack into a machine and having them nailed on. That is the driving method of the manufacture of shoes under these minute subdivisions.

The effect was to multiply production. By 1885 the Massachusetts factories were making four times as many cases of boots and shoes as they had made two decades earlier. The art of shoemaking, as an individual craft, became a thing of the past. The old-time shoe shop, a small room perhaps 10 by 14, disappeared. Remembering how different the workman's life was then, Mr. Eaton said:

In these old shops, years ago, one man owned the shop; he took in work and three, four, five, or six others, neighbors, came in there and sat down and made shoes right in their laps, and there was no machinery. Everybody was at liberty to talk; they were all politicians . . . Of course, under these conditions, there was absolute freedom and exchange of ideas, they naturally would become more intelligent than shoe workers can at the present time, when they are driving each man to see how many shoes he can handle, and where he is surrounded by noisy machinery. And another thing, this nervous strain on a man doing just one thing over and over again must necessarily have a wearing effect on him; and his ideals, I believe, must be lowered.

The shoemakers looked back regretfully on their recent past. It had been the usual practice in those days for cobblers to hire a boy to read aloud from books on philosophy or history or science. It was nothing to interrupt a task in order to debate a fine point in the text. But now "the gentle craft of leather" was gone, and the artisan had become nothing more than "a tender to the machine."

Something of the same nostalgia was voiced by the cigar maker, Samuel Gompers, in his autobiography:

The craftsmanship of the cigar maker was shown in his ability to utilize wrappers to the best advantage, to shave off the unusable to a hairbreadth, to roll so as to cover holes in the leaf and to use both hands so as to make a perfectly shaped and rolled product. These things a good cigar maker learned to do more or less mechanically, which left us free to think, talk, listen, or sing. I loved the freedom of that work, for I had earned the mind-freedom that accompanied skill as a craftsman. I was eager to learn from

An early 19th-century shoe shop. In its one small
room a few craftsmen made the complete shoe in the
days before mass production turned the skilled
worker into a "tender of the machine." (Courtesy
New York Public Library)

discussion and reading or to pour out my feeling in song. Often we chose someone to read to us who was a particularly good reader, and in payment the rest of us gave him sufficient of our cigars so he was not the loser. The reading was always followed by discussion, so we learned to know each other pretty thoroughly. We learned who could take a joke in good spirit, who could marshal his thoughts in an orderly way, who could distinguish clever sophistry from sound reasoning. The fellowship that grew between congenial shopmates was something that lasted a lifetime.

As the brick walls of the factories closed in on them, the workers' sense of personal freedom slipped away. One Massachusetts mechanic in 1879 described the atmosphere in a shop employing 100 to 125 men:

During working hours the men are not allowed to speak to each other, though working close together, on pain of instant discharge. Men are hired to watch and patrol the shop. The workers of Massachusetts have always been law and order men. We loved our country, and respected the laws. For the last five years the times have been growing worse every year, until we have been brought down so far that we have not much farther to go. What do the mechanics of Massachusetts say to each other? I will tell you: "We must have a change. Any thing is better than this. We cannot be worse off, no matter what the change is."

The same worker also said:

I work harder now than when my pay was twice as large. Less than five years ago wages were from $12 to $18 a week currency; now they are from $6 to $12, and work not as steady.

Ten years later, in 1889, the payroll for the Lyman cotton mill in Holyoke, Massachusetts showed wages in the cording room running as low as 5 cents an hour. Here are some samples taken from its ledger:

JOB	TOTAL HOURS	PRICE PER HOUR	WEEKLY AMOUNT
Section Hand	60	$ .20	$12.00
Third Oiler	60	.10	6.00
Scrubber	60	.05	3.00
Picker Man	60	.10	6.00
Stripper	60	.09½	5.70
Lap Oiler	60	.08½	5.10
Grinder	60	.15	9.00
Railways and Drawing	60	.07	4.20

There was a common saying in those days, heard often from housewives: "You go to market with the money in a basket, and carry home the goods in your pocket." To see what a millhand's wages could buy, let's look at these figures on the weekly cost of living taken from a New York labor paper, the *Printer*, August, 1864. These are the actual expenses for a family of six—father, mother, and four children:

Expenditures for the Week

1 bag of flower	$ 1.80
small measure of potatoes daily at 17¢ per day for 7 days	1.19
1/4 pound of tea	.38
1 pound coffee (mixed or adulterated, can't afford better)	.35
3½ pounds sugar	1.05
milk	.56
meats for the week (being on 1/2 ration supply)	3.50
2 bushels of coal	1.36
4 pounds butter	1.60
2 pounds lard	.38
kerosene	.30
soap, starch, pepper, salt, vinegar, etc.	1.00
vegetables	.50
dried apples (to promote health of children)	.25
sundries	.28
rent	4.00
	$18.50

The *Printer* noted the average wage for all branches of the trade locally was $16 a week. (Workers in other trades got as little as $3, $4 or $6 a week.) This family, then, spent $2.50 more than the father earned and had nothing left for clothing or entertainment. The paper added, "The fortunate printer that has more than one suit to his back, or whose wife can boast of more than a change of calicoes, can scarcely be found."

Hours of work were as long as wages were short. The men driving the horse-drawn streetcars of New York City in the 1880s worked 14 to 16 hours a day in all weather. Their pay was $1.75 a day. What it was like to work a 14-hour day is told by Ira Steward, a machinist who devoted his life to the cause of a shorter work week. He wrote in *Fincher's Trades' Review*, October 14, 1865:

Take the average operative or mechanic employed by a corporation 14 hours a day. His labor commences at half-past four in the morning, and does not cease until half-past seven p.m. How many newspapers or books can he read? What time has he to visit or receive visits? to take baths? to write letters? to cultivate flowers? to walk with his family? Will he not be quite as likely to vote in opposition to his real interests as in favor? What is his opinion good for? Will anyone ask his advice? What will he most enjoy, works of art or rum? Will he go to meeting on Sunday? Does society care whether he is happy or miserable? sick or well? dead or alive? How often are his eyes tempted by the works of art? His home means to him his food and his bed. His life is work, with the apparition, however, of some time being without, for his work means bread! "Only that and nothing more." He is debased by excessive toil! He is almost without hope!

Think how monotonous that path leading from house to factory, and from factory to house again—the same sidewalk every day, rain or shine, summer or winter—leading by the same low houses—inhabited by beings walking the same social treadmill as himself. Half-past seven comes at last, and as the wheel stops he catches his coat, and half staggering with fatigue, hurries homeward in the darkness, thinking of nothing but food and rest.

3

WOMEN WHO WORK

"**B**adly as our workmen and mechanics may be treated," said a labor newspaper in 1867, "it is no secret that the condition of females who are obliged to work for a living is far worse."

Manufacturers, always looking for cheap labor, had early found a rich supply in women. They were used to hard work. In the home they put in 12 hours a day or more, cleaning, cooking, sewing, rearing children, helping with the men's chores as well. Their labor was heavy, unending—and unpaid. When employers sent agents into the rural districts to recruit farm girls, thousands responded. The picture of life in the mill towns—high wages, leisure hours, silk dresses—was a promise they could not resist. By 1840 women were in the workshops of a hundred different industries.

But the beauties of factory life proved a myth. Women worked 14 to 16 hours a day for a wage of $1.56 a week.

The Civil War brought many more women into the factories. The number did not shrink after the war, partly because, as one government official put it, women did more and better work than many men who were paid twice as much.

The women who stayed out of the factories and did piece work at home, usually sewing, were no better off. With the invention of the sewing machine, the rates for piece work went down. During the war, umbrella sewers got $3 a week, tassel makers $4, shirtwaist makers 24 cents for a 12-hour day. And the women had to supply their own thread, at 10 cents a spool. In 1870 women were getting 6 cents for each shirt they made. A survey revealed that in New York 7,000 working women could afford to live only in cellars and 20,000 were near starvation.

Often the physical demands of the job were considered too much for the women. In 1875 one supervisor in the printing trades told an investigator for the Massachusetts Bureau of Labor:

I have had hundreds of lady compositors in my employ, and they all exhibited, in a marked manner, both in the way they performed their work and in its results, the difference in physical ability between themselves and men. They cannot endure the prolonged close attention and confinement which is a great part of typesetting. I have few girls with me more than two or three years at a time; they must have vacations, and they break down in health rapidly. I know no reason why a girl could not set as much type as a man, if she were as strong to endure the demand on mind and body.

In the cotton mills of New England and the South tens of thousands of women labored long and dreary hours. Marie Van Vorst, one of the early investigators of labor conditions, went into the South Carolina mills to see what the women did. "Do you like the mills?" she asked. Without exception the answer was, "I hate them." Here is why:

"Spooling" is hard on the left arm and the side. Heart disease is a frequent complaint amongst the older spoolers. The cotton comes from the spinning-room to the spool-room, and as the girl stands before her "side," as it is called, she sees on a raised ledge, whirling in rapid vibration, some one hundred huge spools full of yarn; whilst below her, each in its little case, lies a second bobbin of yarn wound like a distaff.

Her task controls machinery in constant motion, that never stops except in case of accident.

Women and children lugging home loads of material from the general contractor. They did the piece work, usually sewing, in their tenement. (George Eastman House)

With one finger of her right hand she detaches the yarn from the distaff that lies inert in the little iron rut before her. With her left hand she seizes the revolving circle of the large spool's top in front of her, holding this spool steady, overcoming the machinery for the moment not as strong as her grasp. This demands a certain effort. Still controlling the agitated spool with her left hand, she detaches the end of yarn with the same hand from the spool, and by means of a patent knotter harnessed around her palm she joins together the two loosened ends, one from the little distaff and one from this large spool, so that the two objects are set whirling in unison and the spool receives all yarn from the distaff. Up and down this line the spooler must walk all day long, replenishing the iron grooves with fresh yarn and reknitting broken strands . . .

The air of the room is white with cotton, although the spool-room is perhaps the freest. These little particles are breathed into the nose, drawn into the lungs. Lung disease and pneumonia—consumption—are the constant, never-absent scourge of the mill village. The girls expectorate to such an extent that the floor is nauseous with it.

Even the method of payment was degrading, the reporter found:

Some of the hands never touch their money from month's end to month's end. Once in two weeks is payday. A woman had then worked 122 hours. The corporation furnishes her house. There is the rent to be paid; there are also the corporation stores from which she has been getting her food and coal and what gewgaws the cheap stuff on sale may tempt her to purchase. There is a book of coupons issued by the mill owners which are as good as gold. It is good at the stores, good for the rent, and her time is served out in pay for this representative currency. This is of course not oblig-atory, but many of the operatives avail themselves or bind themselves by it. When the people are ill, they are docked for wages. When, for indisposition or fatigue, they knock a day off, there is a man hired especially for this purpose, who rides from house to house to find out what is the matter with them, to urge them to rise, and if they are not literally too sick to move, they are hounded out of their beds and back to their looms.

Believing that working women were defenseless, employers did not hesitate to cheat them. Some brazenly did not pay them at all, and others deducted a large part of the pay for supposedly imperfect work. Here is one woman's account of her experiences:

An ad in a Long Island paper called for a woman to sew on buttons. With glad heart I went, for what could I do better? . . .

After making a satisfactory sample I was told the price was two cents for a gross; no thread supplied. Bewildered, I made some mental multiplication, but I could not think of more than sixty cents for thirty gross of buttons. Of this I subtracted five cents for cotton and thirty cents for car fare, which left a total of twenty-five cents' earnings.

However, I was elated at being of some help, and set to work as soon as I reached home. It took me one whole week to mount the 4,320 buttons, and when I delivered them, using my last five cents for car fare, I was told that only ten gross were mounted properly; that all I could get was thirty cents, and would I call next Saturday.

My next experience was neckties. I made four samples for a firm in Broome Street, which took from 9 o'clock in the morning until 3 o'clock in the afternoon. Then when the fourth bow was finished a pimply-faced young woman approached me with outstretched hand. "One dollar deposit, please," she chirped, and I not having any dollar of which I did not know how to dispose, left this "home-work" place, and also my day's work to its benefit.

No. 3: I furnished a sample, received seventy-five cents' worth of work, and on delivery fifteen cents was taken off for a bow for which I did not get any material, being accused of theft, although not directly.

Another woman, interviewed by the magazine the *Independent*, tells of work in a garment factory in a neighborhood of Brooklyn:

Two years ago I came to this place, Brownsville, where so many of my people are, and where I have friends. I got work in a factory making underskirts—all sorts of cheap underskirts, like cotton and calico for the summer and woolen for the winter, but never the silk, satin, or velvet underskirts. I earned $4.50 a week and lived on $2 a week, the same as before.

I got a room in the house of some friends who lived near the factory. I pay $1 a week for the room and am allowed to do light housekeeping—that is cook my meals in it. I get my own breakfast in the morning, just a cup of coffee and a roll, and at noon time I come home to dinner and take a plate of soup and a slice of bread with the lady of the house. My food for the week costs $1 . . .

I get up at half-past five o'clock every morning and make myself a cup of coffee on the oil stove. I eat a bit of bread and perhaps some fruit and then go to work . . .

At seven o'clock we all sit down to our machines and the boss brings to each one the pile of work that he or she is to finish during the day, what they call in English their "stint." This pile is put down beside the machine and as soon as a skirt is done it is laid on the other side of the machine . . .

The machines go like mad all day, because the faster you work the more money you get. Sometimes in my haste I get my finger caught and the needle goes right through it. It goes so quick though, that it does not hurt much. I bind the finger up with a piece of cotton and go on working. We all have accidents like that. Where the needle goes through the nail it makes a sore finger, or where it splinters a bone it does much harm. Sometimes a finger has to come off. Generally, though, one can be cured by a salve.

All the time we are working the boss walks about examining the finished garments and making us do them over again if they are not just right. So we have to be careful as well as swift.

By 1900 five million women held jobs, two million of them still in domestic service. Nearly one out of every five in the labor force was a woman. Arguments about whether women could or should work were academic. Women knew they were in the working class to stay.

4

CHILDREN IN THE MILLS

"The most beautiful sight that we see is the child at labor," said Asa G. Candler of Atlanta, the founder of Coca Cola. "As early as he may get at labor the more beautiful, the more useful does his life get to be."

Idleness was bad for children, so many people in the nineteenth century believed. And the factory was a God-sent protector against the evils into which idleness might lead children.

In the mills of Paterson, New Jersey the regulations required children to be at work at half-past four in the morning. That was in the 1830s. In Massachusetts about the same time children in the factories worked 12 or 13 hours a day, leaving "little opportunity for daily instruction," a state legislative committee observed. In 1845 the mills in Lowell set hours from sunup to sunset. The work-day in April ran 13 hours and 31 minutes.

It was no handful of children who trudged to the mills at dawn. A New England mechanics' convention estimated in 1832 that about two-fifths of the total number of workers were children.

The census of 1870 reported over 700,000 children between 10 and 15 at work; in 1910, the figure had risen to nearly two million, almost half of whom were girls. This meant that almost one out of every five children in that year worked for wages. Of all those working—children and adults—one out of every 20 was a child.

But the U.S. census figures may well have been too low. In 1890, for example, the federal census reported 5,426 children in the factories of Illinois. But when the state investigated the factories four years later, they found more children than that in a check of just 15% of the factories. About one worker in 10 was under 16.

The work children performed was of all kinds, from making artificial flowers in their own tenement flats to tending rows of machines in huge factories.

In 1877 the *Labor Standard* described the breaker room in the Hickory Colliery, near St. Clair, Pennsylvania:

In a little room in this big, black shed—a room not twenty feet square—forty boys are picking their lives away. The floor of the room is an inclined plane, and a stream of coal pours constantly in. They work here, in this little black hole, all day and every day, trying to keep cool in summer, tying to keep warm in winter, picking away among the black coals, bending over till their little spines are curved, never saying a word all the livelong day. These little fellows go to work in this cold dreary room at seven o'clock in the morning and work till it is too dark to see any longer. For this they get $1 to $3 a week. Not three boys in this roomful could read or write. Shut in from everything that is pleasant, with no chance to learn, with no knowledge of what is going on about them, with nothing to do but work, grinding their little lives away in this dusty room, they are no more than the wire screens that separate the great lumps of coal from the small. They had no games; when their day's work is done they are too tired for that. They know nothing but the difference between slate and coal.

Almost 30 years later, in 1906, John Spargo visited the coal mines and described in greater detail the boys he found in the breakers:

Work in the coal breakers is exceedingly hard and dangerous. Crouched over the chutes, the boys sit hour after hour picking out the pieces of slate and other refuse from the coal as it rushes past to the washers. From the cramped position they have to assume, most of them become more or less deformed and bent-backed like old men. When a boy has been working for some time and begins to get round-shouldered, his fellows say that "He's got his boy to carry round wherever he goes."

The coal is hard, and accidents to the hands, such as cut, broken, or crushed fingers, are common among the boys. Sometimes there is a worse accident: a terrified shriek is heard, and a boy is mangled and torn in the machinery, or disappears in the chute to be picked out later smothered and dead. Clouds of dust fill the breakers and are inhaled by the boys, laying the foundations for asthma and miners' consumption.

I once stood in a breaker for half an hour and tried to do the work a twelve-year-old boy was doing day after day, for ten hours at a stretch, for sixty cents a day. The gloom of the breaker appalled me. Outside the sun shone brightly, the air was pellucid, and the birds sang in chorus with the trees and the rivers. Within the breaker there was blackness, clouds of deadly dust enfolded everything, the harsh, grinding roar of the machinery and the ceaseless rushing of coal through the chutes filled the ears . . .

From the breakers the boys graduate to the mine depths, where they become door tenders, switch-boys, or mule-drivers. Here, far below the surface, work is still more dangerous. At fourteen or fifteen the boys assume the same risks as the men, and are surrounded by the same perils. Nor it is in Pennsylvania only that these conditions exist. In the bituminous mines of West Virginia, boys of nine or ten are frequently employed. I met one little fellow ten years old in Mt. Carbon, W. Va., last year, who was employed as a "trap boy." Think of what it means to be a trap boy at ten years of age. It means to sit alone in a dark mine passage hour after hour, with no human soul near; to see no living creature except the mules as they pass with their loads, or a rat or two seeking to share one's meal; to stand in water or mud that covers the ankles, chilled to the marrow by the cold draughts that rush in when you open the trap-door for the mules to pass through; to work for fourteen hours— waiting—opening and shutting a door—waiting again— for sixty cents; to reach the surface when all is wrapped in the mantle of night, and to fall to the earth exhausted and have to be carried away to the nearest "shack" to be revived before it is possible to walk to the farther shack called "home."

No observer could write of these children without commenting almost at once on the effect of their labor upon their health and their spirit. Take Mary Jensen, a New York City child, whose story was told by Robert Hunter in the magazine *World's Week* in 1905:

When I heard of her she was nine years old, and she lived in the basement of a big East Side tenement. She was born in poverty and fed at starving breasts until she was old enough to be laid on the floor in a bundle of rags, watched by her older sister while the mother went out to clean offices downtown. To her the state of hunger seemed normal, and if she had had in these early days a full meal it would doubtless have made her ill. She was a poor, weak, frail little thing, seemingly with almost bloodless veins. Before she was four she had exhausted her play time. She was of those too poor to be assured of that "inalienable" right of childhood, and her little fingers were taught to twist papers and wires into artificial flowers. As long as hands could be kept at it she twisted these materials and formed from them sprigs of blossoms, and as soon as a few dozen were finished her older sister hurried off to get a few pennies for coffee and bread.

A child in a cellar, without food and without the wholesome fatigue that comes from out-door play, needs little rest; and so these little hands worked on until night and stopped only when the mother's mind was eased from the fear and dread of the landlord, who came with clock-like regularity and stormed and cursed and threatened eviction when the rent was not paid.

A few years later Mary was sent out to a candy factory, where she dipped candy six days a week, from seven in the morning until seven at night. When the Christmas season came round she worked longer, sometimes 78, 79, and 80 hours a week. She hardly knew that this great season meant for many children glowing fires, warm logs, toys, and stockings, and candy, and loving words, and a jolly, open-hearted, open-handed, child-loving Santa Claus. She only knew that when this season came she had to hurry to make candy which she never ate, and her little neighbors were compelled to hurry and work late in making toys, flowers and other things which they themselves were never to enjoy. Mary's eyes grew tired and blurred, her little body was shaken—first with a bronchitis—and then came a more stubborn cough that racked all her little frame. The drug-store medicines failed to bring relief, and during the following year the life which had meant for this child but little else than hunger and toil slowly ebbed away.

In 1883 a committee of the U.S. Senate, investigating "the relations between labor and capital," looked into child labor in the cotton mills. One of those it took testimony from was Thomas L. Livermore, manager of the Amoskeag mills in Manchester, New Hampshire:

QUESTION: *Won't you please tell us your experience with the question of child labor; how it is, and to what extent it exists here; why it exists, and whether, as it is actually existing here, it is a hardship on a child or on a parent; or whether there is any evil in that direction that should be remedied?*

ANSWER: *There is a certain class of labor in the mills which, to put it in very common phrase, consists mainly in running about the floor—where there is not as much muscular exercise required as a child would put forth in play, and a child can do it about as well as a grown person can do it—not quite as much of it, but somewhere near it, and with proper supervision of older people, the child serves the purpose. That has led to the employment of children in the mills, I think . . .*

Now, I think that when it is provided that a child shall go to school as long as it is profitable for a workman's child (who has got to be a workingman himself) to go to school, the limit has been reached at which labor in the mills should be forbidden. There is such a thing as too much education for working people sometimes. I do not mean to say by that that I discourage education to any person on earth, or that I think that with good sense any amount of education can hurt any one, but I have seen cases where young people were spoiled for labor by being educated to a little too much refinement.

Mr. Livermore need have had no fear that the children might become a little too refined to be useful in the mills. Twenty years later, in 1903, Marie Van Vorst found children five, six and seven years old amid the looms of South Carolina's mills:

Through the looms I catch sight of Upton's, my landlord's, little child. She is seven; so small that they have a box for her to stand upon. She is a pretty, frail, little thing, a spooler—"a good spooler, tew!" Through the frames on the other side I can only see her fingers as they clutch at the flying spools; her head is not high enough, even with the box, to be visible. Her hands are fairy hands, fine-boned, well-made, only they are so thin and dirty, and nails—claws: she would do well to have them cut. A nail can be torn from the finger, is torn from the finger frequently, by this flying spool. I go over to Upton's little girl. Her spindles are not thinner nor her spools whiter.

"How old are you?"

"Ten."

She looks six. It is impossible to know if what she says is true. The children are commanded both by parents and bosses to advance their ages when asked.

"Tired?"

She nods, without stopping. She is a "remarkable fine hand." She makes 40 cents a day. See the value of this labor to the manufacturer—cheap, yet skilled; to the parent it represents $2.40 per week . . .

Besides being spinners and spoolers, and weavers even, the children sweep the cotton-strewed floors. Scarcely has the miserable little object, ragged and odorous, passed me with his long broom, which he drags half-heartedly along, than the space he has swept up is cotton-strewn again. It settles with discouraging rapidity; it has also settled on the child's hair and clothes, and his eyelashes, and this atmosphere he breathes and fairly eats, until his lungs become diseased . . .

Here is a little child, not more than five years old. The land is a hot enough country, we will concede, but not a savage South Sea Island! She has on one garment, if a tattered sacking dress can so be termed. Her bones are nearly through her skin, but her stomach is an unhealthy pouch, abnormal. She has dropsy. She works in a new mill—in one of the largest mills in South Carolina. Here is a slender little boy—a birch rod (good old simile) is not more slender, but the birch has the advantage: it is elastic—it bends, has youth in it. This boy looks ninety. He is a dwarf; twelve years old, he appears seven, no more. He sweeps the cotton off the floor of "the baby mill." (How tenderly and proudly the owners speak of their brick and mortar.) He sweeps the cotton and lint from the mill aisles from 6 P.M. to 6 A.M. without a break in the night's routine. He stops of his own accord, however, to cough and expectorate—he has advanced tuberculosis.

At night the shanties receive us. On a pine board is spread our food—can you call it nourishment? The hominy and molasses is the best part; salt pork and ham are strong victuals.

It is eight o'clock when the children reach their homes—later if the mill work is behind-hand and they are kept over hours. They are usually beyond speech. They fall asleep at the table, on the stairs; they are carried to bed and there laid down as they are, unwashed, undressed; and the inanimate bundles of rags so lie until the mill summons them with its imperious cry before sunrise, while they are still in stupid sleep.

That was a Southern mill. But it was not much different in the North as is quite evident from the reports of John Spargo, who studied New England's factories in 1906. Around 1900 it was estimated that at least 80,000 children, most of them little girls, were employed in the country's textile mills.

Pennsylvania, whose industrial conditions had earned it the title of "that state of colossal industrial crimes," had 120,000 children working in its mines and mills in 1900. The state's silk mills and lace factories employed 17,000 girls under 16, many of them working from 6:30 at night until 6:30 the next morning. Children as young as six labored in New Jersey's glass factories. Thousands more worked in that state's tobacco and cigar factories. In New York State, the 1900 census reported there were 92,000 children under 15 at work.

Witnesses have described the effects upon health of long hours of hard work. Some kinds of work were in themselves more harmful than others. Laundries, bakeries, saloons, hotels, restaurants were usually unsanitary, badly ventilated or put children in harmful company. Other occupations were a direct physical danger: the railroads, the mines and quarries, glass factories, sawmills, iron and steel mills, stockyards, tobacco factories.

There was still another way these children were injured. Their school days were over when they walked into the factory. With no future chance to learn, the doors to a better life were shut. Their labor was a dreary road ended only by injury, sickness or age.

5

TENEMENTS AND SWEATSHOPS

Be a little careful, please! The hall is dark and you might stumble over the children pitching pennies back there. Not that it would hurt them; kicks and cuffs are their daily diet. They have little else. Here where the hall turns and dives into utter darkness is a step, and another and another. A flight of stairs. You can feel your way, if you cannot see it. Close? Yes! What would you have? All the fresh air that ever enters these stairs comes from the hall-door that is forever slamming, and from the windows of dark bedrooms that in turn receive from the stairs their sole supply of the elements God meant to be free, but man deals out with such niggardly hand.

That was a woman filling her pail by the hydrant you just bumped against. The sinks are in the hallway, that all the tenants may have access—and all be poisoned alike by their summer stenches. Hear the pump squeak! It is the lullaby of tenement-house babies. In summer, when a thousand thirsty throats pant for a cooling drink in this block, it is worked in vain. But the saloon, whose open door you passed in the hall, is always there. The smell of it has followed you up.

Here is a door. Listen! That short hacking cough, that tiny helpless wail—what do they mean? They mean that the soiled bow of white you saw on the door downstairs will *have another story to tell—Oh! a sadly familiar story—before the day is at an end. The child is dying with measles. With half a chance it might have lived; but it had none. That dark bedroom killed it . . .*

We grope our way up the stairs and down from floor to floor, listening to the sounds behind the closed doors— some of quarreling, some of coarse songs, more of profanity. They are true. When the summer heats come with their suffering they have meaning more terrible than words can tell. Come over here. Step carefully over this baby—it is a baby, in spite of its rags and dirt—under these iron bridges called fire-escapes, but loaded down, despite the incessant watchfulness of the firemen, with broken household goods, with washtubs and barrels, over which no man could climb from a fire. This gap between dingy brickwalls is the yard. That strip of smoke-colored sky up there is the heaven of these people. Do you wonder the name does not attract them to the churches?

That baby's parents live in the rear tenement here. She is at least as clean as the steps we are now climbing. There are plenty of houses with half a hundred such in. The tenement is much like the one in front we just left, fouler, closer, darker—we will not say more cheerless. The word is a mockery. A hundred thousand people lived in rear tenements in New York last year. Here is a room neater than the rest. The woman, a stout matron with hard lines of care in her face, is at the washtub. "I try to keep the children clean," she says, apologetically, but with a hopeless glance around. The spice of hot soapsuds is added to the air already tainted with the smell of boiling cabbage, of rags and uncleanliness all about. It makes an overpowering compound. It is Thursday but patched linen is hung upon the pulley-line from the window. There is no Monday cleaning in the tenements. It is washday all the week round, for a change of clothing is scarce among the poor.

That was a glimpse of life in a New York tenement, seen through the eyes of a great reporter, Jacob Riis. He published his indictment of slum conditions in 1890 in a book called *How the Other Half Lives*. With his pencil and camera he pried into the darkest corners of the slums, walking up and down the East Side streets at all hours of the day and night, studying the system "that was the evil offspring of public neglect and private greed."

It was the greed of the landlord that fostered the slum, said Riis. The profit maker "saw in the homeless crowds from over the sea only a chance for business, and exploited them to the uttermost, making sometimes a hundred percent on the capital invested—always most out of the worst houses, from the tenants of which 'nothing was expected' save that they pay the usurious rents."

Many of the tenements were workshops as well as homes, soon tagged "sweatshops." How these came into being is told by Samuel Gompers in his autobiography:

In 1871 and 1872 many Bohemians moved into downtown New York. The Bohemians did not find it easy to learn English or to adjust themselves to New York life. As many manufacturers thought they had an advantage in the mold and filler system under which practically unskilled workers could produce cigars, soon they added the tenement feature which was an entirely different method from the old home work or factory work. The manufacturers bought or rented a block of tenements and subrented the apartments to cigar makers who with their families lived and worked in three or four rooms. The cigar makers paid rent to their employer for living room which was their work space, bought from him their supplies, furnished their own tools, received in return a small wage for completed work sometimes in script or in supplies from the company store on the ground floor. The whole family—old and young had to work in order to earn a livelihood—work early and late, Sunday as well as Monday. The system was degrading to employer and workman. It killed craft skill and demoralized the industry.

That system of "home work" spread rapidly to other trades, especially to the making of clothing. Its effect on the working family's life is reported by John DeWitt Warner in *Harper's Weekly* in 1895:

The first contractor sublets the work to a "sweater," whose shop is generally one of the two larger rooms of a tenement flat, accommodating from six to fifteen or twenty "sweating" employees—men, women, and children. In the other large room of the flat are his living, sleeping, and cooking arrangements, overflowing into the workroom. Employees whom he boards, who eat at their work, and who sleep on the goods, frequently complete the intimate connection of home and shop. One-fourth of our ready-made and somewhat of our custom-made clothing are thus put together.

The people engaged are those whose families are most prolific, whose sense of cleanliness is least developed, who comprehend no distinction between living and work rooms, whose premises are dirty to the point of filth, and who are found in the most densely populated portions of the city.

But this is not the worst. Single families, inhabiting one or more rooms, generally having a family as subtenants, or a number of lodgers or boarders, subcontract work from the tenement "sweaters." Thus by tenement "homeworkers" are made another one-fourth of our ready-made clothing and a much larger proportion of our children's clothing. The homes of these homeworkers include many of the most wretched in which human beings exist among us. The conditions of squalor and filth are frequently such as to make even inspection impossible, except by one hardened to the work, while the quarters in which this work is centered are those into which tend the most helpless of our population.

From the wholesale manufacturer, handling each year a product of millions, through the contractor to the "sweater," and on to the "homeworker," the steps are steadily downward—of decreasing responsibility, comfort, and compensation. The profit of each (except the wretch at the bottom) is "sweated" from the next below him.

The contractors' shops are much like other factories—the large proportion of foreign labor and a tendency toward long hours being their main distinctions. In the tenement "sweatshops" unhealthy and unclean conditions are almost universal, and those of filth and contagion common. The employees are in the main foreign-born and newly arrived. The proportion of female labor is large, and child labor is largely used. Wages are from a fourth to a third less than in the larger shops. As to hours, there is no limit except the endurance of the employees, the work being paid for by the "task," and the task so adjusted as to drive from the shop any employee who, whenever he is given a bench, will not work to the limit of physical endurance, the hours of labor being rarely less than twelve, generally thirteen or fourteen, frequently from fifteen to eighteen hours in the twenty-four.

The lot, however, of these "sweatshop" workers is a luxury compared to that of those engaged in tenement homework. The homeworker is generally a foreigner just arrived, and frequently a woman whose husband is dead, sick, or worthless, and whose children keep her at home. Of these tenement homeworkers there are more women than men, and children are as numerous as both. The work is carried on in the one, two, or three rooms occupied by the family, with its subtenants or boarders. No pretence is made of separating shop work from household affairs. The hours observed are those which endurance alone limits. Children are worked to death beside their parents. Contagious diseases are especially prevalent among these people; but even death disturbs from their occupation only the one or two necessary to dispose of the body.

As to wages in this "tenement homework," there is nothing which can properly be so called. The work is secured by underbidding of tenement sweatshops, and is generally piece-work, one process of which may be attended to by the head of the family, and the rest by its other members according to their capacity. Those engaged are so generally compelled to accept rather than to choose their work that it is taken without reference to the possibility of gaining a livelihood therefrom, the miserable workers earning what they can, begging to supplement it, and dying or being supported as paupers when they fail.

A large proportion—nearly, if not quite, one-half—of all the clothing worn by the majority of our people is thus made under conditions revolting to humanity and decency, and such as to endanger the health of the wearer.

How much did these sweatshop workers earn? Jacob Riis finds out:

Turning the corner into Hester Street, we stumble upon a nest of cloak-makers in their busy season. Six months of the year the cloak-maker is idle, or nearly so. Now is his harvest. Seventy-five cents a cloak, all complete, is the price in this shop. The cloak is of cheap plush, and might sell for $8 or $9 over the store-counter. Seven dollars is the weekly wage of this man with wife and two children, and $9.50 rent to pay per month. A boarder pays about a third of it. There was a time when he made $10 a week and thought himself rich. But wages have come down fearfully in the last two years. Think of it: "come down" to this.

The other cloak-makers aver that they can make as much as $12 a week, when they are employed, by taking their work home and sewing till mid-night. One exhibits his account with a Ludlow Street sweater. It shows that he and his partner, working on first-class garments for a Broadway house in the four busiest weeks of the season, made together from $15.15 to $19.20 a week by striving from 6 A.M. to 11 P.M., that is to say, from $7.58 to $9.60 each. The sweater on this work probably made as much as 50 per cent at least on their labor. Not far away is a factory in a rear yard where the factory inspector reports teams of tailors making men's coats at an average of 27 cents a coat, all complete except buttons and buttonholes.

Was it any different for workers' families in other cities? The Citizens' Association of Chicago investigated the tenement areas of that city in 1883–1884. Their report told of

the wretched condition of the tenements into which thousands of workingmen are huddled, the wholesale violation of all rules for drainage, plumbing, light, ventilation and safety in case of fire or accident, the neglect of all laws of health, the horrible conditions of sewers and outhouses, the filthy, dingy rooms into which they are crowded, the unwholesome character of their food, and the equally filthy nature of the neighboring streets, alleys and back lots filled with decaying matter and stagnant pools.

For these pigsties, said the report, working-class families were "fleeced at a rate which returns 25 to 40 per cent per annum of the value of the property."

Turn to Boston and the same conditions are seen. The North End was the first place the poorest immigrants came to, crowding into tenement houses vacated by the more skilled workers able to move up the economic ladder. Most of the houses were once for single families, but now several families were jammed into the filthy, foul-smelling homes where they shared common privies and washrooms. The dirty, twisted alleys were dumping grounds. Sickness and death took high toll among the slum dwellers.

In New York, a Tenement House Commission looked into the effects of the slums upon children. In homes such as these, children were "damned rather than born" into the world. The worst of these tenements it called "infant slaughter houses," for they killed one in every five babies born into them.

The facts are plain in the story recounted by Jacob Riis of just one city block. Bear in mind that the term "child" here means any person under five years of age. Everyone older was figured an adult.

In this block between Bayard, Park, Mulberry and Baxter Streets, "the Bend" proper, the late Tenement House Commission counted 155 deaths of children in a specimen year (1882). Their percentage of the total mortality in the block was 68.28, while for the whole city the proportion was only 46.20. The infant mortality in any city or place as compared with the whole number of deaths is justly considered a good barometer of its general sanitary conditions. Here, in this tenement, No. 59½, next to Bandits' Roost, fourteen persons died that year, and eleven of them were children; in No 61 eleven, and eight of them not five years old. According to the records in the Bureau of Vital Statistics only thirty-nine people lived in No. 59½ in the year 1888, nine of them little children. There were five baby funerals in that house the same year. Out of the alley itself, No. 59, nine dead were carried in 1888, five in baby coffins.

No attention was paid by most manufacturers to the way their workers lived. By 1890, according to one estimate, 10% of the population in the big cities was housed in slums as bad as those of the worst places in Europe. Near every factory, stockyard or mine were huddled the ugly tenements or shacks of the workers. Millions of slum dwellers were immigrants. Because they were poor they had to live in the heart of the city or industrial community. They clung together to be close to the people whose customs and language they knew. Their colonies were often in the worst, most criminal and politically corrupt parts of the city. In Baltimore 77% of the slum population was of foreign birth or parentage in 1894. In Chicago it was 90%, in Philadelphia 91%, in New York 95%.

The slums became "wildernesses of neglect," as Robert Hunter put it, "almost unexplored and almost unknown" to the people on the upper side of society. It was a sorry school for the immigrant to learn what America was and what it stood for.

6

WHO OWNS AMERICA?

It is 1884.

Imagine yourself getting an invitation to a dinner party from one of New York's wealthy gentlemen. It is to be given at Delmonico's, the favorite restaurant of the rich. This is how you are entertained that night, according to press reports:

The table was constructed with a miniature lake in the center thirty feet in length, enclosed by a network of golden wire which reached to the ceiling, forming a great cage. Four immense swans were secured from one of the parks and placed in this lake. High banks of flowers of every hue surrounded the lake and covered the entire table, leaving barely enough room for the plates and wine glasses. The room was festooned with flowers in every direction. Miniature mountains and valleys with carpets of flowers made vocal with sparkling rivulets, met the eye on every hand. Golden cages filled with sweet singing birds hung from the ceiling and added their enchantment to the gorgeous spectacle. Soft, sweet music swept in from adjoining rooms, and all that art, wealth and imagination could do was done to make the scene one of unexampled beauty. And then the feast! All the dishes which ingenuity could invent or the history of past extravagance suggest, were spread before the guests. The oldest and costliest wines known to the trade flowed like the water that leaped from the cascades

in the banqueting hall. The guests were wild with exulta-
tion and delight and tarried far into the night.

About the same time a New York newspaper surveyed
the unemployed and the poor of the city and found 150,000
persons were out of work. Another 150,000 earned less
than 60 cents per day, many of them girls who worked 11
to 16 hours daily. During the course of the year over 23,000
of the city's families were evicted from their homes because they could not pay the rent.

The Delmonico display was soon to be outdone. In 1897
the Bradley Martins gave a ball at the Waldorf Astoria
Hotel in New York. As one of the family described it:

The interior was transformed into a replica of Versailles
and rare tapestries, beautiful flowers, and countless lights
made an effective background for the wonderful gowns and
their wearers. I do not think that there has ever been a
greater display of jewels before or since; in many cases the
diamond buttons worn by the men represented thousands
of dollars and the value of the historic gems worn by the
ladies baffles description. My sister-in-law impersonated
Mary Stuart and her gold embroidered gown was trimmed
with pearls and precious stones. Bradley, as Louis XV,
wore a suit of gold brocade ... The suit of gold inlaid armor
worn by Mr. Belmont was valued at ten thousand dollars.

There was so much money at the disposal of the rich
they filled their teeth with diamonds, spent $75,000 for a
pair of opera glasses and $65,000 for a dressing table. A
pet poodle wore a diamond collar worth $15,000, and a host
offered his guests cigarettes wrapped in hundred dollar
bills. Impatient to become cultured overnight, a copper
king bought himself a complete museum of art.

In 1861 the country could boast only a handful of men
who commanded such wealth, but by 1892 a New York
newspaper was able to count more than 4,000 millionaires
in the United States.

In that great revolution based upon the machine and
the factory, the poor had also multiplied many times over.
In 1890, of the country's 12.5 million families, 11 million

had an average income of $380 a year. The richest 1% of the country enjoyed wealth greater than the total of the remaining 99%. As one historian said, "Never before or since in American history have the rich been so rich and the poor so poor." Perhaps one example will show what he was getting at. In Chicago, Marshall Field paid the best workers in his giant department store $12 for a 59-hour week. Mr. Field himself pocketed $600 every hour of the 24-hour day, every day of the 365-day year.

It was Mark Twain who gave the late 19th century the name that has stuck—the Gilded Age. This was a country, he said, tongue in cheek, "where there is no fever of speculation, no inflamed desire for sudden wealth, where the poor are all simpleminded and contented, and the rich are all honest and generous, where society is in a condition of primitive purity, and politics is the occupation of only the capable and the patriotic."

Twain was joking, but Andrew Carnegie—who drew $25 million a year from his giant steel mills—was not when he defied any man to show there were paupers in the United States. From his palace on Fifth Avenue he could not see Potters Field, where one out of every ten persons who died in Manhattan was being buried.

Carnegie was only one of business's great captains. There were Philip Armour, James Hill, Jay Gould, Jim Fisk, John D. Rockefeller, J.P. Morgan. These men who were to form "the new nobility of industry and banking" had most of them reached their maturity in the Civil War. Few if any fought in that war; like J.P. Morgan, they used the Draft Act provision allowing them to pay $300 for a man to fight in their place. "Only greenhorns enlist," Judge Mellon of Pittsburgh wrote his son James. "Here there is no credit attached to going. All stay if they can and go if they must. Those who are able to pay for substitutes do so and no discredit attached."

So the young Mellons and Morgans stayed and carried their flags to the economic battleground. "Get money— honestly if you can, but at any rate get money!" That, said Henry George, was the lesson society was daily and hourly dinning into every ear. It was a lesson J.P. Morgan absorbed, as he showed when he bought for $17,500 a store of government-owned rifles condemned as defective and sold them back to the government the next day for $110,000.

The getting of material wealth became the highest goal of life. The desire for money possessed almost all Americans. There was a headlong rush to grab new markets and drive out competitors from the old. In a fever of speculation Americans sank their money into the wildest schemes. The salesman and the promoter took over. Like Morgan, many of the leaders of the new post–Civil War generation earned their original capital as commission merchants during the war.

The training some of them got was realistic. Rockefeller's father, a lumber dealer, moneylender and seller of patent medicines, said: "I cheat my boys every time I get a chance. I want to make 'em sharp. I trade with the boys and skin 'em. I just beat 'em every time I can. I want to make 'em sharp."

The policy that produced their great wealth was simple. James B. Duke of the American Tobacco Company said it: "First, you hit your enemies in the pocketbook, hit 'em hard. Then you either buy 'em out or take 'em in with you."

Nothing must interfere with the need to make a profit. Even religion, these men believed, had its profitable side. *The Law of Success*, a book issued by the Southern Methodist Publishing House in 1885, spoke of "the commercial value of the Ten Commandments" and suggested that the educator of the future "teach his pupils what will pay best. He will teach them the art of thinking, which, for the purpose at hand, I may define to be the art of turning one's brains into money."

From the Civil War on, business grew larger and larger, and as the money power merged with the industrial power, it grew more unified. *Monopoly*—the domination or control of a whole industry such as steel or oil by one company—took hold, and the trusts soon followed.

Jay Gould was one of the men who typified that age. Although he was not the most powerful of the titans, he was a symbol to the people of his own time. The son of a poor New York State farmer, he was on his own at 16, out to make his fortune quickly. The great size of a prospect dazzled him, and in the development of the early railroads he found his opportunity. By the late 1880s he had acquired the Union Pacific, the Wabash, the Missouri-Kansas-Texas and the Texas-Pacific, as well as several smaller Eastern railroads. Looking beyond the railroads, he took over the Western Union Telegraph Company, the New York *World*, several steamship lines and coal mines, and the new rapid transit lines of New York City. His method was to get working control of ruined properties, usually by manipulating stocks, and with small expense turn them to his own profit for a time and then get out just as the property failed again. By such means he made $20 million on the Union Pacific alone.

So legendary were his exploits that doggerel circulated celebrating "Jay Gould's Modest Wants":

> *My wants are few; I scorn to be*
> *A querulous refiner;*
> *I only want America*
> *And a mortgage deed of China;*
> *And if a kind fate threw Europe in,*
> *And Africa and Asia,*
> *And a few islands of the sea,*
> *I'd ask no other treasure,*
> *Give me but these—they are enough*
> *To suit my notion—*
> *And I'll give up to other men*
> *All land beneath the ocean.*

Gould's behavior won notice even in a popular boy's magazine of the period:

> *Of course we all knew it was not a square game,*
> *But show me the man who would not do the same.*

The Gilded Age could almost be said to have been the railroad age. The rails ran across everything—industry, technology, agriculture, politics, morals. The linking of the two oceans by the transcontinental railroad at Promontory Point, Utah in 1869 was a landmark not only of great technical achievement but of the time's corruption. The businessmen who promoted it spent twice the maximum amount per mile of construction that the engineers had estimated was possible. And when the road was done, over $50 million could not be accounted for.

The "empire builders" had made and used friends in high places all along the way—from a speaker of the house and future president, James A. Garfield, to a future vice president, Schuyler Colfax. Senators, congressmen and cabinet officials were welcomed into their holding company, the Credit Mobilier, into which the profits from the juicy construction contracts flowed for redistribution. Made stockholders for little or nothing, the politicians passed laws and appropriation bills benefiting what was now their own property. Because of the operations of the new tycoons, many a political leader emerged a millionaire.

"Steal largely or not at all," was the advice of the robber barons, "for it is preached in Gotham that he who steals largely and gives donations to the Church shall enter the kingdom of heaven, while to him who confines his stealings to modest peculations shall be opened the doors of Sing Sing."

The bribe had become the custom in political life. The vote of the legislator was for sale like any other product. The corporations and trusts dominated everything.

What was the trust? James B. Weaver, a general in the Union Army, gave his energies after the Civil War to attacks upon political corruption and to exposure of of the new trusts. In his book, *A Call to Action*, he described the trust:

Trust is defined to be a combination of many competing concerns under one management. The object is to increase profits through reduction of cost, limitation of product and increase of price to the consumer. The term is now applied, and very properly, to all kinds of combinations in trade which relate to prices, and without regard to whether all or only part of the objects named are had in view . . .

Trusts vary somewhat in their forms of organization. This is caused by the character of the property involved and the variety of objects to be attained. The great trusts of the country consist of an association or consolidation of a number of associations engaged in the same line of business—each company in the trust being first separately

The satiric weekly Puck *had a strong notion of who wielded the real influence on government, as shown in t#is detail from Keppler's drawing, "Bosses of the Senate."* (Courtesy New York Public Library)

incorporated. The stock of these companies is then turned over to a board of trustees who issue back trust certificates in payment for the stock transferred. The trust selects its own board of directors and henceforth has complete control of the entire business and can regulate prices, limit or stimulate production as they may deem best for the parties concerned in the venture. The trust itself is not necessarily incorporated. Many of the strongest, such as the "Standard Oil Trust," the "Sugar Trust," and the "American Cotton Seed Oil Trust" and others are not. They are the invisible agents of associated artificial intangible beings. They are difficult to find, still harder to restrain and so far as present experience has gone they are practically a law unto themselves.

The power of these institutions has grown to be almost incalculable.

Some verses of the day told the story of a man who saw a great factory, and asking whose it was, was told, "It's Morgan's." A railroad turned out to be Morgan's too, and so did a vast fleet of ships:

> *I dwelt in a nation filled with pride;*
> *Her people were many, her lands were wide;*
> *Her record in war and science and art*
> *Proved a greatness of muscle and mind and heart.*
> *"What a great old country it is!" I cried;*
> *And a man with his hat in the air replied:*
> *"It's Morgan's."*

For a time everyone believed he could become his own Morgan. There were "acres of diamonds" to be picked up right in your own backyard, a Baptist minister said. In a famous lecture of that title, Russell H. Conwell preached the gospel of wealth over 6,000 times to audiences all over the country. "Success was an outward sign of inward grace," he said, and continued:

Never in the history of the world did a poor man without capital have such an opportunity to get rich quickly and honestly as he has now.

I say that you ought to get rich, and it is your duty to get rich. How many of my pious brethren say to me, "Do you, a Christian minister, spend your time going up and down the country advising young people to get rich, to get money?" "Yes, of course I do." They say, "Isn't that awful! Why don't you preach the gospel instead of preaching about man's making money?" "Because to make money honestly is to preach the gospel." That is the reason. The men who get rich may be the most honest men you find in the community . . .

Ninety-eight out of one hundred of the rich men of America are honest. That is why they are trusted with money. That is why they carry on great enterprises and find plenty of people to work with them. It is because they are honest men . . .

Some men say, "Don't you sympathize with the poor people?" Of course I do . . . But the number of poor who are to be sympathized with is very small. To sympathize with a man whom God has punished for his sins, thus to help him when God would still continue a just punishment, is to do wrong, no doubt about it, and we do that more than we help those who are deserving. While we should sympathize with God's poor—that is, those who cannot help themselves—let us remember there is not a poor person in the United States who was not made poor by his own shortcomings, or by the shortcomings of some one else. It is all wrong to be poor, anyhow.

No one seemed immune to the corruption of a money society. Reverend Henry Ward Beecher, the most noted preacher of that time, took a thousand dollar fee to endorse a trust, but there were no outcries against it. Nor were disapproving voices raised when he pocketed $15,000 worth of stock from Jay Cooke in return for printing favorable editorials in the *Christian Union* about Cooke's Union Pacific Railroad.

Collis P. Huntington, promoter of the Southern Pacific, used public officeholders as errand boys in behalf of his railroads. Bribery was only in the line of his duty, he believed, and in a letter of 1877 he set forth his plain thinking:

If you have any money to have the right thing done, it is only just and fair to do it . . . If a man has the power to do great evil and won't do right unless he is bribed to do it, I think the time spent will be gained when it is a man's duty to go up and bribe the judge. A man that will cry out against them himself will also do these things himself. If there was none for it, I would not hesitate.

Working as a clerk in Washington for a petty income he never made from his *Leaves of Grass*, Walt Whitman saw what was happening to his America. "The depravity of the business classes of our country," he wrote in 1871, "is not less than has been supposed, but infinitely greater."

The poet saw how money was being worshiped: "Democracy looks with suspicious, ill-satisfied eyes upon the very poor, the ignorant, and on those out of business. She asks for men and women with occupations, well-off, owners of houses and acres, and with cash in the bank."

And Mark Twain, toward the end of the Gilded Age, commented, "The political and commercial morals of the United States are not merely food for laughter, they are an entire banquet."

Some of the rich professed the same piety as the Reverend Conwell. Rockefeller, the genius of that age of trust organization, thought of himself as merely the custodian of wealth. "I believe the power to make money is the gift of God . . . to be developed and used to the best of our ability for the good of mankind."

That, Mr. Dooley, a fictional philosopher, replied, makes the rich "a kind iv a society f'r th' previntion iv croolty to money."

Others were not at all pious. Take Vice President Galloway of the Manhattan Elevated Railroad Company. When someone protested that the elevated road was encroaching on his property, Galloway replied defiantly: "We have the legislature on our side, the courts on our side, and we hire the law by the year."

Just as blunt was one millionaire of the 1880s who said, "We are the rich; we own America; we got it, God knows how, but we intend to keep it if we can."

7

BREAD OR BLOOD

Those were gaudy times for the men who knew they owned America.

But their "Great Barbecue"—as Mark Twain called it—was never enjoyed by the workers who dug the wealth out of the mines or sweated it out of the mills. With an almost fatal rhythm, depression after depression came along to throw millions out of work. Hard times hit in 1867, in 1873, in 1884, in 1893, in 1907 . . . All were bitter disasters for the workers and their families, whether the crisis lasted a year or many years.

To see what hard times meant, let's look at the depression that began in September 1873. It was one of the biggest and worst. It grew deeper and deeper, until by 1877 it had engulfed nearly all but the rich.

What brought it on? Many of the same causes that lie behind every depression. In their race for profits, businessmen poured money recklessly into mines, mills and railroads. A furious pace of growth was forced by the craze for speculation. Many investors sank their money into projects that demanded huge sums of capital, but that could not bring returns for years to come. Eager to keep profits high, business overproduced in every market and squeezed workers' wages to the lowest possible level. As goods poured out of the factories at lower and lower costs, employers pocketed the profits instead of sharing them with the workers through higher wages and lower hours.

Or they plowed profits back into still greater production. The masses of the people lacked the buying power the national economy needed to maintain its prosperity.

When the big banking house of Jay Cooke collapsed in 1873, the economy toppled. Down came hundreds of other banks and businesses. Panic spread swiftly. The men, women and children suddenly vanished from the long aisles of the textile mills; the clacking looms fell silent. Miners climbed up out of the earth and left gaping holes empty for years to come. Farmers walked out of their fields and the plows rusted alone.

What had wrecked so many lives overnight seemed a mystery. No crop failure, no insect invasion, no "act of God" had harmed the huge stores of food and clothing. Weren't the wheat and cotton still there, and the iron and coal and oil? Why then were millions of strong workers, able to bring in the harvests and sew the clothing and mine the earth, standing on street corners begging for food and shelter?

A New York labor paper, the *Toiler*, reported:

Thousands of homeless men and women are to be seen nightly sleeping in the seats in the public parks, or walking the streets . . . The suffering next winter will be tremendous . . . Three thousand boys and girls applied at the 6th Ward Station House for tickets for the poor children's excursion; scarcely one of them had shoes or hats, and half were naked.

When the first shock came that September, it was thought times would soon be better. But things grew worse and worse all through October. By November the misery was widespread. In New York, the public charities were besieged by sufferers. The streets swarmed with beggars. The police stations and the charity lodging houses were thrown open and packed nightly with the homeless. By December over 100,000 men, women and children were idle, many of them homeless and hungry. By January the city heard of one death and then another and another and another from starvation. A relief society reported that "50,000 people are living by charity or beggary and 10,000 homeless men and women are in the streets." One wealthy New Yorker, a Mr. Bennett, opened up soup kitchens, and every day from 12 to 14 thousand applicants for relief swarmed in.

That first winter of the depression 20,000 paraded in Chicago, demanding "bread for the needy, clothing for the naked, and houses for the homeless." The city would spend nothing. At the mayor's request, $700,000 was doled out to the needy from a private fund collected for the victims of the Chicago fire.

Some of those better off called the unemployed "lazy, idle, worthless loafers, frauds, blackguards, and Irishmen." But John Swinton, an editor of the New York *Sun* who studied the scene, wrote:

Take the records of but a single soup kitchen and free lodging house—that in Leonard Street, for the last month. In that month among the applicants registered you will find 398—what? Loafers? No! carpenters. And 383— what? Thieves? No! painters. And 234—what? Blackguards? No! printers. 80 bookbinders, 132 shoemakers, 132 tailors, 67 hatters, 80 jewelers and watchmakers, 98 tinsmiths, 61 harnessmakers, 112 blacksmiths, 216 puddlers, 139 boilermakers, 77 engineers, 143 moulders, 105 brass-finishers, 97 gasfitters, and many workers at other mechanical pursuits, to the number in all of over 3,000. Are such men—and this report is a fair specimen of the reports—loafers, vermin, outlaws, or outcasts? We hear also that many of the recipients of relief were men who refused work at fair wages. You must judge whether it be just to say such things of our mechanics and laborers, or whether such men actually prefer the humiliation of idle pauperism to the pride of industrious independence. It is false to them, to human nature, and to all our experience in the city, to say that they do.

That same week the freight handlers of the Erie Depot struck for $2 pay for a 10-hour day, and their places were at once taken by men eager to scab for 17 cents an hour, or some $8 or $9 a week. The Erie manager said that he could easily get 5,000 men on the same terms.

As winter came on and New York did nothing for the unemployed, the bitter workers tried to make city officials and the prosperous classes understand the degree of suffering. At a meeting of the unemployed held in Cooper Union in December, placards spelled out their misery:

7,500 LODGED IN OVERCROWDED CHARNEL
STATION HOUSES PER WEEK

10,000 HOMELESS MEN AND WOMEN
IN OUR STREETS

20,850 IDLE MEN FROM 11 TRADE UNIONS,
ONLY 5,950 EMPLOYED

110,000 IDLE OF ALL CLASSES
IN NEW YORK CITY

182,000 SKILLED UNION WORKMEN IDLE
IN NEW YORK STATE

Then, with still nothing being done to help, plans were made for a gigantic parade to Tompkins Square that would climax in a demand for a public works program. After much trouble, permission was given to demonstrate, and Mayor Havemeyer promised to address the meeting. The night before, however, the police board changed its mind and canceled the permit so suddenly the workingmen could not be notified.

That morning of January 13, 1874, the demonstrators began to gather in the square, bearing signs proclaiming:

THE UNEMPLOYED DEMAND WORK,
NOT CHARITY

WHEN THE WORKINGMEN BEGIN TO THINK,
MONOPOLY TREMBLES

No policemen were stationed at the square to tell the demonstrators of the revoked permit or to warn them back. But at 10 o'clock, as 50,000 people stood peaceably awaiting the arrival of the mayor, platoons of police rushed into the square. What happened is described by John Swinton:

Suddenly a great cry arose, and the blanched faces of many of the men hemmed in the crowd showed they thought the time had come. The alarm extended through the neighborhood, and the excitement was fearful. The police, with drawn batons, were closing in on all sides, and a terrible encounter seemed probable. The rear rank in a moment afterward faced about, and in an instant both ranks charged in opposite directions. The squad under command of Sergeant Kass did quick work. That under Sergeant Berghold met with more opposition. The sight of blood increased the fury of the gathering, and the policemen's clubs were freely used. The mounted squad did effective work . . . The reporter . . . saw a great cloud of dust arising in the neighborhood of the mounted police, and a rush of men and boys, nearly frantic, through Eighth Street from the Square. The rapidly retreating crowd did not look behind. They simply yelled and moved as fast as their legs could carry them. Captain Speight's men were close at their heels, their horses galloping at full speed on the sidewalks. Men tumbled over each other into areas or into the gutters, or clambered up high stoops to get out of the way of the chargers. The horsemen beat the air with their batons, and many persons were laid low. There seemed to be a determination on the part of the mounted police to ride over somebody, and they showed no mercy. There was no use in attempting to resist the horsemen. One policeman actually rode into a grocery and scattered the terrified inmates.

At a signal from the Captain the horsemen again took to the sidewalks with their steeds, and calm and interested spectators of a moment before were flying as though before a whirlwind. The reserves, having been deployed, made an onslaught upon the outer edge of the crowd, while the men in the station charged out. Taken thus in front and rear, the multitude melted. A few that could not run well were assisted in their flight by blows from the locusts of police, who struck vigorously at shoulders and limbs. It took hardly a minute to clear sidewalks and streets. An im-

mense throng had collected in Fifth Street, east of Second. Another charge was ordered, and the crowd were soon flying, with the police mercilessly clubbing them in the rear. They were not permitted to assemble again, and policemen were stationed at a few yards distance from each other, and every time half a dozen men halted together, they were charged upon, and blows from clubs were administered even before orders to move on were given.

Year after year the depression went on. By 1877 one out of five workers was jobless, and two out of five worked no more than half the year. That winter the count of unemployed stood at three million.

Legions of the unemployed drifted across the country, hunting for work. They slept in barns and hayricks, in boxcars and under bridges, on park benches or in hallways. In the cold months they sought the big cities, often committing petty thefts that would land them in warm jails. When spring came on they took to the road again. As the years of desperation hardened them, they grew less peaceable. The newspapers and the police cried out ceaselessly against these "tramps," calling them thieves or communists. They were tagged enemies of society, religion and property. No matter how many laws were passed against vagrancy, there seemed to be no end to the "tramp evil."

Only one-fifth of the workers in the United States were left with steady jobs. And for them, wages were cut as much as 50%, often to as little as a dollar a day. In New York's building trades, artisans who had earned $2.50 for an eight-hour day in 1872 had to accept $1.50 for a 10-hour day in 1875. Railroad workers lost 30 to 40% of their pay, and furniture workers as much as 60%.

Labor did not take the wage cuts quietly at first. Strikes erupted here and there, but with two men standing by for every job, the strikes were quickly lost. When one Chicago lumber worker killed himself, a newspaper noted: "No cause, except despondency caused by poverty, was assigned." In Chicago's streets a banner flew at the head of a marching column of demonstrators. BREAD OR BLOOD read the grim slogan.

8

I LOVE THIS UNION CAUSE

WELCOME TO THE SONS OF TOIL FROM NORTH, SOUTH, EAST AND WEST! proclaimed the banner stretched across the Baltimore convention hall that hot August day in 1866.

It was only a year since the victory at Appomattox. But that year "the new birth of freedom" had seen strikes and lockouts, the jailing of labor leaders and the slaughter of blacks in the streets of Memphis and New Orleans. Everywhere employers were getting together to beat off labor's demand for better wages and shorter hours. In Boston and Buffalo, New York and St. Louis, the new tycoons had formed local associations, and nationally the stove manufacturers and the iron founders had set an example by founding trade associations.

A labor paper in Rochester, New York warned in 1866:

Capital is centralizing, organizing, and becoming more powerful every day. The late war and what has grown out of the war, made capital stronger. It has made millions, all at the expense of the labor of this country, and the capital thus concentrated is to be used in a greater or less degree to defeat the objects sought by the workingmen.

Another labor paper asked:

What must we workers do to combat the stranglehold of
capital? We must unite ourselves in a union of unions . . .
and establish a national labor federation . . . Thus, we will
present a solid front to our enemies and cement the unity
among the workingclass throughout the nation.

As far back as the 1790s workers had begun to form local
unions as the only way to protect themselves against the
abuses of employers. The basic idea was group action.
Alone, no worker was a match for the boss. Joined in a
union, workers had power to bargain on more equal terms
with an employer. For a long time the workers had sensed
the need to go beyond local action and form national
organizations. They tried to do it in the 1830s, 1840s and
1850s. But conditions were not yet ripe. Now, with the
country's industrial power rocketing and with business
operating on a national scale, the time had come. At
Baltimore the 77 delegates from 13 states formed the
National Labor Union (NLU). One estimate held there
were about 200,000 workers organized in some 300 local
unions.

From their seats the delegates chanted:

Whether you work by the hour or work by the day,
Decreasing the hours increases the pay.

The jingle voiced their chief demand. The eight-hour
movement had been launched in 1863 by Ira Steward, the
Massachusetts machinist, and had swiftly won the support of millions. If you cut the hours without cutting the
pay, he argued, you would need a bigger labor force to do
the work. That would mean more buying power, which
would raise production, end depressions and give working
people the time for rest, recreation and education.

The delegates in Baltimore whooped through the eight-
hour resolution, declaring it would "free the labor of this
country from capitalistic slavery."

The convention said it was the urgent duty of every
worker to join a union, and where none existed, to start
one. It called on the unions to unite in local, national and
international bodies in every trade. It deplored the use of

strikes, except as a last resort, proposing that arbitration be used instead.

But how was the eight-hour day to be secured? The National Labor Union had one answer—political action through the formation of labor's own national party. The foremost spokesman for a labor party was the National Labor Union's leader, William H. Sylvis. A small but muscular iron molder with blond hair and blue eyes, he was the founder of one of the first national unions in his own trade, as well as of the National Labor Union. Now 38, he had spent the last 10 years of his life organizing. "I love this union cause!" he said. "I hold it more dear than my family or my life. I am willing to devote to it all that I am or hope for in this world."

Hounded by bill collectors and hardly able to feed his wife and five children, he went from city to city, telling workers everywhere, "Singlehanded we can accomplish nothing, but united there is no power of wrong that we cannot openly defy." To factory after factory he went, welding the workers into closed shops, rousing the hatred of employers, one of whom warned him:

The day is not far distant when the conditions of work-ingmen will be worse than ever before. The day will come when men who are now active in the labor movement will be forced upon their bended knees to ask for work . . . A spirit of retaliation has been aroused in the bosom of every employer, the fruits of which are now being manifested in the widespread and universal organization of capitalists for the avowed purpose of destroying your unions.

Behind the eight-hour movement tremendous pressure was generated. In 1868 Congress passed an eight-hour law for government workers, and so did five states. The unions rejoiced—briefly, for experience soon taught them the laws were full of holes designed to let employers work the labor force 10 hours or more through special contracts.

Sylvis argued:

We have tried the balance-power or make-weight expe-dient of questioning candidates, and throwing our votes in

favor of such as indorsed or were pledged to our interests.
How vain and futile this expedient has proven is known to
all. It is but a history of broken promises and violated
pledges and invariably ends in exposing our weakness; for
say what you will, men of opposite opinions to the
candidate's will not trust him in the face of such frequent
deceptions . . . If we resort to political action at all, we must
leap clear of entangling alliances. With a distinct
workingman's party in the field, there can be no distrust,
no want of confidence. When it becomes a fixed fact that
workingmen can vote for men of them and with them, the
incentive will be sufficient to unite the masses in one grand
struggle for victory. We should then know for whom and
for what *we voted. Every toiler would feel that he held his*
destiny in his own hands.

He also wanted the National Labor Union to join the
International Workingmen's Association, formed in
London in 1864 chiefly through the efforts of Karl Marx.
"Our aims, interests and objects are the same everywhere," Sylvis told the National Labor Union. An international alliance "would destroy the power of the
capitalists to supplant workingmen struggling for their
rights in one portion of the world by the importation of
help from another . . . Our cause is a common one! It is
a war between poverty and wealth; labor occupies the
same low position and capital is the same tyrant in all
parts of the world." The National Labor Union sent a
delegate abroad and exchanged correspondence with the
international leaders.

Just as important to labor's strength was solidarity with
women who worked, thought Sylvis. Most unions barred
women from membership, but Sylvis did not hesitate to
challenge the prejudice:

As men struggling to maintain an equitable standard of
wages and to dignify labor, we owe it to consistency, if not
to humanity, to guard and protect the rights of female
labor, as well as those of our own . . . How can we hope to
reach the social elevation for which we all aim without
making women the companion of our advancement?

Four women delegates were welcomed to the National Labor Union's 1868 congress, and Kate Mullaney, head of the Laundry Workers Union in Troy, New York, was made assistant secretary and national organizer of women.

The question of black labor came up at a convention. Just before the meeting, the National Labor Union put out this address to workers:

Negroes are four million strong and a greater proportion of them labor with their hands than can be counted from among the same number of other people on earth. Can we afford to reject their proffered cooperation and make them enemies? By committing such an act of folly we would inflict greater injury upon the cause of labor reform than the combined efforts of capital could accomplish . . . So capitalists North and South would foment discord between the whites and blacks and hurl one against the other as interest and occasion might require to maintain their ascendancy and continue the reign of oppression.

It was an explosive issue. Race prejudice, rampant in the North as well as the South, had built an iron ring of law and custom around the African American. It had made him a second-class citizen denied the rights and privileges every American was entitled to.

Appealing for unity, the address went on:

What is wanted is for every union to help inculcate the grand ennobling idea that the interests of labor are one; that there should be no distinction of race or nationality; no classification of Jew or Gentile, Christian or infidel; that there is one dividing line, that which separates mankind into two great classes, the class that labors and the class that lives by others' labor.

The question was debated at the convention, but a declaration deferred. Sylvis opposed putting it off, but he was unable to break down the prejudice. White artisans feared the competition of skilled black workers and kept them out of their crafts and unions.

At the 1869 convention of the National Labor Union nine black delegates were finally seated, and one of them, Isaac Myers of Baltimore, representing the Colored Caulkers' Trades Union Society, made this appeal to the convention:

I speak for the colored men of the whole country . . . when I tell you that all they ask for themselves is a fair chance; that you shall be no worse off by giving them that chance; that you and they will dwell in peace and harmony together; that you and they may make one steady and strong pull until the laboring men of this country shall receive such pay for time made as will secure them a comfortable living for their families, educate their children and leave a dollar for a rainy day and old age. Slavery, or slave labor, the main cause of the degradation of white labor, is no more. And it is the proud boast of my life that the slave himself had a large share in the work of striking off the one end of the fetters that bound him by the ankle, and the other that bound you by the neck.

Employers, sharing the same race prejudice as the workers, did not draw the color line if it helped them to weaken the white unions. Northerners imported southern blacks to force down wages and break unions. The effect was of course to sharpen the split between black and white workers.

The militant black leader, Frederick Douglass, saw his son Lewis, a Civil War veteran, jim crowed by the Washington branch of the International Typographical Union. In a letter to the *New York Times* in 1869, the father took the case to the public:

[Lewis] is made a transgressor working at a low rate of wages by the very men who prevented his getting a high rate. He is denounced for not being a member of a Printers' Union by the very men who would not permit him to join such a Union. He is not condemned because he is not a good printer, but because he did not become such in a regular way, that regular way being closed against him by the men now opposing him.

*Suppose it were true that this young man had worked
for lower wages than white printers receive, can any printer
be fool enough to believe that he did so from choice? What
mechanic will ever work for low wages when he can possi-
bly obtain higher? Had he been a white young man, with
his education and ability, he could easily have obtained
employment, and could have found it on the terms demanded by the Printers' Union.*

There is no disguising the fact—his crime was his color.

Refusing to wait until whites were ready to invite them
into their unions, blacks organized themselves. In 1867
several strikes by black labor broke out in the South. (The
very word "strike" was still so new that some newspapers
put it into quotes; it was not yet part of the accepted
language.) In Charleston black longshoremen won higher
wages, and in New Orleans white laborers joined blacks
on the levee and in a two-hour strike forced a better pay
scale. In Savannah dock workers, mostly blacks, won a
strike that ended a poll tax on all wharf workers.

After the National Labor Union convention of 1869, in
which black delegates were at last seated, the carpenters
and joiners decided to take down their barrier against
blacks, but few other unions were ready to follow.

Later in 1869 blacks formed the National Colored Labor
Union and elected Isaac Myers president.

William Sylvis began to think the only way out for
workers was to get rid of the wage system. Let the workers
set up their own cooperatives, said the head of the National Labor Union, and "divide the profits among those
who produce them." But cooperatives proved no answer in
a world dominated by private corporations and banks. The
union workshops could not compete with powerful industries and soon almost all of them failed.

Although it petered out as a debating society for reformers, the National Labor Union in its brief six years pion-
eered in building a national federation of unions, in
fighting for the eight-hour day, for the rights of women
and the rights of blacks, and in organizing the unorganized.

9

REBELLION
ON THE RAILROADS

The great depression of the seventies destroyed most of the trade unions. In 1877 the New York *Commercial and Financial Chronicle* assured its readers that "Labor is under control for the first time since the war."

But the paper spoke too soon. That was to be the year of the most violent labor upheaval of the century. It was the Railway Strike of 1877, the first great collision between American capital and labor.

It had not been long in the making. Railroads had etched the map of the new industrial society in scarcely half-a-dozen years. Thirty-three thousand miles of track were laid between 1867 and 1873, spurred on by the vast grants of federal and state credit and lands.

When the panic of 1873 broke, the railroads suffered like everything else. As the depression spiraled downward, roads went bankrupt. Profits could be kept up only by ruthless economies and ruthless competition.

Wage rates were cut 35% in three years, so that management could continue to squeeze out dividends of 8 to 10%. Grievances mounted among the workers. The lines of job seekers lengthened outside the hiring offices. Those still on the job had to work 15 to 18 hours a day—and then wait three or even four months to collect earnings that were due monthly. On the Erie, trackmen who had traditionally squatted free in shanties along the line, were now forced to pay rent or get out. Some railroads even took away the passes the men needed to ride to and from their jobs. Sometimes they had to pay more to ride back to their homes than they had earned to run the train out. And living expenses in railroad-owned hotels away from home were so high that workers sometimes were left with as little as 35 cents for a day's work.

In May 1877, the Pennsylvania put through a new 10% wage cut, and the men accepted it. On top of that, it ordered doubleheading, which meant one crew had to take out twice as many cars as before. So for even less pay they did double the work—and saw half the other workers fired.

Then, on July 11, the unpredictably explosive move was made. The Baltimore & Ohio announced a 10% cut too. The workers protested. Under the new scale, a fireman would get only $1.50 a day. How could he support a family on $6 a week (he worked only four days weekly) and take care too of his living expenses away from home? But management was deaf. Quit if you like, it replied; we can always replace you.

They quit. On July 16, the day the new scale went into effect, 40 firemen and brakemen refused to work. They were replaced, and the trains started to move. It wasn't the first time a tiny rebellion had flared and been stamped out. But this time a great flame roared up as from a deep slumbering volcano. At Martinsburg, West Virginia trainmen seized the depot and said no freights would leave until their wage cut was restored. The railwaymen's women stood by them. The Baltimore *Sun* took special note of their spirit:

The singular part of the disturbances is the very active part taken by the women, who are the wives and mothers of the firemen. They look famished and wild, and declare for starvation rather than have their people work for the reduced wages. Better to starve outright, they say, than to die by slow starvation.

The Baltimore & Ohio then insisted that the governor request federal troops from President Rutherford B.

As the great railroad strike of 1877 spread from city to city, troops were called out to make the trains move. On July 20 in Baltimore the Sixth Maryland militia fired on a workers' demonstration and killed 12 people. (Courtesy New York Historical Society)

Hayes. Through his secretary of war, the president ordered 400 soldiers to Martinsburg. From the train the reporter for the New York *World* wrote:

It has been well observed that if the rights of the strikers had been infringed or violated instead of that of the railroad corporations, it is probable that Governor Matthews would have hesitated a long while before he would have thought it his duty to call on the president for aid.

Meanwhile, trouble was racing along the tracks. At nearly every important rail center in the country strikes broke out. At Pittsburgh on July 19, the Pennsylvania's trainmen took over the switches and the depot and refused to let freight trains move. The sheriff read the strikers the riot act, but the men stood firm. The governor sent in the county's militia—who promptly joined the strikers. When 600 troops ordered up from Philadelphia arrived in Pittsburgh, they marched straight into a demonstration of men, women and children. Stones were thrown and the soldiers fired; 26 people were killed and many more badly wounded. A grand jury inquiry called the shooting "an unauthorized, willful, and wanton killing . . . which the inquest can call by no other name but murder."

The New York *Herald's* reporter wrote:

The sight presented after the soldiers ceased firing was sickening. Old men and boys attracted to the [scene] . . . lay writhing in the agonies of death, while numbers of children were killed outright. Yellowside, the neighborhood of the scene of the conflict, was actually dotted with the dead and dying; while weeping women, cursing loudly and deeply the instruments which had made them widows, were clinging to the bleeding corpses.

Enraged, the crowd, swelled by thousands of workers from the rolling mills, factories and coal mines, attacked the militia so fiercely that it was forced to seek shelter in the roundhouse. The citizens—now 20,000 strong—had seized arms and munitions and captured three pieces of artillery from the state troopers. They ran a carload of oil-soaked coke up against the roundhouse and set the building aflame. The besieged troops shot their way out and fled the city. Burning and looting went on all night, destroying some $5 million worth of railroad property.

Strikes flared up in New York along the tracks of the Erie and the Central. The militia was called out, but it fraternized with the workers. One officer of the 69th New York regiment said:

Many of us have reason to know what long hours and low pay mean and any movement that aims at one or the other will have our sympathy and support. We may be militiamen, but we are workmen first.

Moving west, trouble broke out in Toledo, Columbus, Cincinnati, St. Louis, Chicago. Everywhere militia and federal troops aided by vigilantes fought strikers and rioters.

The grim reality of this open warfare stunned many Americans standing on the sidelines. Historian James Ford Rhodes, who lived through it, said:

We had hugged the delusion that such social uprisings belonged to Europe and had no reason of being in a free republic where there was plenty of room and an equal chance for all.

From the beginning most of the press had called it a communist conspiracy to overthrow the government by force and violence. (The Paris Commune of 1871 was still a frighteningly fresh memory.) "The mob is a wild beast and needs to be shot down," said the New York *Herald.* CITY IN POSSESSION OF COMMUNISTS was the *New York Times* headline in Chicago. The New York *Sun* called for "a diet of lead for the hungry strikers." It was echoing Tom Scott, head of the Pennsylvania Railroad, who advised giving the strikers "a rifle diet for a few days and see how they like that kind of bread."

But the Pennsylvania legislature, after a long investigation of the strike, reported:

The railroad riots of 1877 have by some been called an insurrection. They were not a rising against civil or political authority; in their origin they were not intended by their movers as an open and active opposition to the execution of the law . . . It was in no case an uprising against the law as such . . . There was a sort of epidemic of strikes running through the laboring classes of the country, more particularly those in the employ of large corporations, caused by the general depression of business, which followed the panic of 1873, by means whereof many men were thrown out of work, and the wages of those who could get work were reduced.

In Chicago, the *Daily News* was able to look calmly into the background of the strike and declare:

For years the railroads of this country have been wholly run outside the United States Constitution . . . They have charged what they pleased for fare and freight rates. They have corrupted the State and city legislatures. They have corrupted Congress employing for the purpose a lobby that dispensed bribes to the amount of millions and millions . . . Their managers have been plundering the roads and speculating on their securities to their own enrichment. Finally, having found nothing more to get out of the stockholders . . . they have commenced raiding not only upon the general public but their own employees.

With the strike still on, a large and fashionable audience assembled on Sunday in Plymouth Congregational Church in Brooklyn to hear what their pastor, the Reverend Henry Ward Beecher, had to say about the nationwide disorder. As the New York Times noted, he found a special kind of humor in it:

It is true that $1 a day is not enough to support a man and five children, if a man insists on smoking and drinking beer. Is not a dollar a day enough to buy bread? Water costs nothing. (Laughter.) Men cannot live by bread, it is true; but the man who cannot live on bread and water is not fit to live. (Laughter.) When a man is educated away

from the power of self-denial, he is falsely educated. A
family may live on good bread and water in the morning,
water and bread at midday, and good water and bread at
night. (Continued laughter.) Such may be called the bread
of affliction, but it is fit that man should eat of the bread
of affliction . . . The great laws of political economy cannot
be set at defiance.

Ministers of such prosperous congregations were usually chosen because their training, special position and
associations made it likely they would hold the same
opinions as their parishioners. So too with judges. Railroads seeking to protect themselves against labor's demands knew they could count on a sympathetic
interpretation of property rights. Supreme Court Justice
Samuel F. Miller commented in 1875:

It is vain to contend with judges who have been at the
Bar the advocates for forty years of railroad companies,
and all the forms of associated capital, when they are called
upon to decide cases where such interests are in contest. All
their training, all their feelings are from the start in favor
of those who need no such influence.

Judges and ministers might take the side of the railroad
owners, but public feeling ran the other way. The New
York Tribune noted that "the manifestations of public
opinion are almost everywhere in sympathy with the
insurrection." Sympathy with the strikers was the other
face of hatred for the railroads. Pittsburgh, where the
citizens wrecked the railroad's property, was proof
enough. The people had suffered from four terrible years
of depression. They understood the railroad workers'
grievances. They felt the same bitterness and discontent.
They would not stand by and watch government troops
offer bullets in place of bread. They demonstrated with the
strikers and fought to defend them from the troops. Some
there were who approved of the strike but not the rioting.
Others, however, went further: "Of course the strikers
must carry their point," said one man, ". . . I don't care how
much railroad property they burn; it will teach these

monopolists a lesson." And a Scranton paper, the Republican, said, "The popular heart is sound. It is full of warnings to the corporations to adopt a wiser and kindlier policy in their dealings with their employees." "I talked to all the strikers I could get my hands on," a Pennsylvania militiaman wrote home, "and I could find but one spirit and one purpose among them—that they were justified in resorting to any means to break down the power of corporations."

By August 2, the national wave of strikes was over, crushed by police, vigilantes and government troops. But in the two weeks it lasted, the workers had stopped most of the traffic on two-thirds of the nation's 75,000 miles of track. The railroad men had come close to winning. Some of the roads had canceled their wage cuts to forestall a strike. Others had quickly given in to the strikers' demands. But enough held out to exhaust the strength of a movement that had no funds and no central leadership. When the peak of the riots was past, the roads brought in strikebreakers, and the ranks of the strikers crumbled. The workers' only hope had been to panic the managers into quick settlement. When that failed, it was the end.

The end of their jobs, too, for many strikers. The Burlington fired 131 men because they had struck, and many other roads did the same. But the *New York Times* did not see the great strike itself as a failure:

The workmen have here and there compelled compliance with their demands, and in other instances they have attracted popular attention to their grievances, real or alleged, to an extent that will render future indifference impossible . . . The balance of gain is on the side of the workmen.

The nation's business leaders drew a lesson from the universality of the strike. *Iron Age* summed it up:

One point is probably settled for the present at least; the reduction in the wages of labor has reached its lowest point . . . It would be a bold step in a wrong direction to give notice of a decrease in wages.

The strike called a halt to industry's relentless wage cutting. Now managers knew their men had real grievances that must be listened to. Workers were not dirt or stone, but human beings with dignity and pride.

10

DREAM—AND REALITY

As business picked up in 1879, a new wave of immigrants began rolling from the far-off corners of Europe to the United States. In the decade beginning in 1880, over half a million a year landed in the promised land. They came to escape conscription and war, to find decent wages and equality, to know freedom and justice for the first time.

How they came and what they found was described by John Swinton in 1883:

The contractors make their appearance under the American flag among the half-starved mudsills in the most wretched districts of Hungary, Italy and Denmark, tell the stories of fabulous wages to be gotten in America, bamboozle the poor creatures, rope them in and make contracts with them to pay their passage across the sea, upon their agreeing to terms that few can understand. When they reach the districts of this country to which the contractors ship them, they find their golden dreams turned into nightmares, as they are put to work in mines, factories, or on railroads, at even lower wages than those of them whom they throw out of work.

Why industry systematically hired immigrants is revealed in a report on the Carnegie Steel Company in Pittsburgh, issued by the Sage Foundation:

It is a common opinion in the districts that some employ-
ers of labor give the Slavs and Italians preference because
of their docility, their habit of silent submission . . . and
their willingness to work long hours and overtime without
a murmur. Foreigners as a rule earn the lowest wages and
work the full stint of hours . . .
    Many work in intense heat, the din of machinery and the
noise of escaping steam. The congested conditions of most of
the plants in Pittsburgh add to the physical discomforts . . .
while their ignorance of the language and of modern ma-
chinery increases the risk. How many of the Slavs, Lithuani-
ans and Italians are injured in Pittsburgh in one year is
unknown. No reliable statistics are compiled . . . When I
mentioned a plant that had a bad reputation to a priest he
said: "Oh, that is the slaughter-house; they kill them there
every day." . . . It is undoubtedly true, that exaggerated though
the reports may be, the waste in life and limb is great, and if
it all fell upon the native-born a cry would long since have
gone up which would have stayed the slaughter.

The plant owners used many of the immigrants as
strikebreakers. In the 1870s and 1880s, Swedish, German
and Italian immigrants were brought into the bituminous
coal fields to break strikes. "All I want in my business is
muscle," a California employer said. "I don't care whether
it be obtained from a Chinaman or a white man, from a
mule or a horse!"
    In 1882 the coal miners in the Pittsburgh district issued
an appeal against the practice, condemning:

The enticing of penniless and unapprised emigrants,
speaking uncommon languages and just landed at Castle
Garden, to the mines to undermine our wages and social
welfare, and to take the place of our workmen.
    The quartering and restraining of these emigrants in huts
and shanties far within their property line for the sole pur-
pose of preventing them and the old miners from holding joint
meetings, where all the facts, reasons and objects of this
resistance could be fully stated and fairly discussed . . .
    The object of this capitalistic assault is to check our
growth, undermine our strength and destroy District No.

9; and if the operators succeed in breaking up our Assemblies and our District with cheap immigrant labor, it will encourage and lead them to use the same tactic to defeat and destroy other Districts of the Order.

In the iron and steel mills too, foreign labor was imported. The differences in culture and language made it hard for the unions to organize the newcomers. The employers encouraged a constant war of nationalities. The immigrants were not told they were to serve as strikebreakers before they arrived on the scene. Often their baggage was taken away as security for the repayment of loans advanced for transportation.

Prejudice against immigrants developed rapidly among the workingmen's organizations. The Chinese in the West were among the first victims of racism. They had come first in the fifties, to work in the goldmines. After the Civil War they helped build the railroads and harvest the crops, working for lower wages. Fury against them mounted in the depression of the seventies. They were the victims of lynchings and mass riots. By the early 1890s Congress had passed a series of laws keeping out almost all Chinese. The labor unions played a big part in putting up the barriers.

The arguments against the Chinese, condemning them as racially inferior, began to reach other immigrants, too. The earlier wave of immigration, between 1820 and 1860, had come from Great Britain and northern and western Europe. Now, as the 1880s saw the immigrants from eastern and southern Europe begin to outnumber the earlier arrivals, uneasiness spread.

All through the seventies and into the eighties, railroads and manufacturers continued to bring in contract labor. In 1884 Congressman Foran, once a union leader, introduced a bill to ban the import of alien labor under contract. It became law the next year and was strengthened several times later on. A powerful force for its passage was the Knights of Labor, now the nation's leading labor organization.

The Knights of Labor had been formed in 1869 by a Philadelphia garment cutter, Uriah Stephens. A strictly secret organization, surrounded by ritual, it grew only

Prejudice against immigrant workers found an
early target in the Chinese. Some were beaten
or murdered; many had their homes looted and
burned. In 1880 in Denver a racist mob savagely
attacks the Chinese and wrecks their homes.
(Courtesy New York Historical Society)

slowly during the depression years. By 1878, with 10,000 members, it had established a national footing and adopted a program.

The Knights' platform advocated arbitration instead of strikes; the eight-hour day, wherever possible; an end to the contract labor system, convict labor and child labor; the passage of health and safety legislation; and equal pay for equal work done.

Monopoly was evil, the Knights believed; the way to get rid of it was through government ownership of railroads, telephones and telegraphs, which would lead some day to a cooperative society.

T. V. Powderly, a mild and dapper little Irish mechanic and a superb orator, became the Knights' leader, and under public pressure the order soon abandoned its secrecy. Powderly dreamed of a classless society and dreaded the strife between labor and capital. He disapproved of strikes, boasting that the Knights had never called one while he was in command.

In many places the Knights of Labor organized local labor assemblies that took in semiskilled and unskilled workers, and blacks without any reservations. The trade unions had failed to organize the unskilled, even though they were by now perhaps 70% of all labor.

In the eighties the Knights' slogan—AN INJURY TO ONE IS THE CONCERN OF ALL—rallied thousands of workers to join their ranks. They struck too, for often they had no other way of winning recognition. Powderly still deplored this, preferring to educate the country into his new cooperative society. But if any measure of justice and equality was to be had, the workers found they had to fight their way to it.

Another depression hit the country in 1883. It lasted less than two years, but the industrialists again tried to slash wages to keep profits up. The chief victims were the semiskilled and unskilled workers. Bitter and angry, they set off a wave of strikes early in 1884. And again, as in the seventies, employers fought back with every weapon. Imported strikebreakers, labor spies, blacklists, state militias and yellow-dog contracts were used to break the strikes. Toward the year's end, labor turned to the boycott, starting hundreds of them. The list of products workers were asked not to buy became long enough to fill a fat catalog. Many of the boycotts were successful.

By now all kinds of workers were drawn into militant action. Strikes by quarrymen, lumbermen, bricklayers and street railroadmen drew national attention. The Knights of Labor won an unplanned strike against Jay Gould's Union Pacific Railroad, forcing it to cancel a 10% wage cut. Three months later the railroad workers tied up the line again and stopped another wage reduction. Powderly was still deploring strikes, but the rank and file were joining the picket lines all the same.

The next year the workers on three more of Gould's lines struck to protest a 10% wage cut and won immediate victory. Five months later, the Wabash Line began to fire men active in the Knights' local assemblies. Failing to settle it by arbitration, the Knights ordered all its members on Gould's roads to refuse to repair or handle the rolling stock of his Wabash line. Gould—who had boasted, "I can hire one half the working class to kill the other half"—caved in at the threat; he could not afford a stoppage on 20,000 miles of his rails. It was a complete victory for the Knights of Labor, a victory that made them the leaders of the labor movement.

Now there was a mad rush to join the order. From 100,000 members in mid-1885, the Knights leaped to 700,000 a year later. They became page one news and a force whose favor legislators rushed to win. State after state—except in the South—began to bar the sale of goods made by convict labor at low wages in competition with free labor. Contract labor was banned by Congress, which also set up a Federal Bureau of Labor in 1884. By 1900, 30 states had established similar agencies, giving labor the official recognition won earlier by business and agriculture.

The first report issued by Federal Labor Commissioner Carroll D. Wright showed just where the worker stood in 1886. If the country wants to know, said Wright, "whether the wage-worker received his equitable share of the benefit derived from the introduction of machinery, the answer must be no."

People arriving from Europe often had no place to stay until they could find jobs and a place to live. In New York City Italian immigrants were put up in these bare barracks. (George Eastman House, photo by Lewis W. Hine)

The average worker brought home a wage of $7.50 to $8.00 a week. What this meant to a family was told in 1883 to the Senate Committee on Labor-Capital Relations by Thomas O'Donnell, a Fall River textile worker:

I have a brother who has four children besides his wife and himself. All he earns is $1.50 a day. He works in the iron works at Fall River. He only works nine months out of twelve. There is generally three months of stoppage . . . and his wife and family all have to be supported for a year out of the wages of nine months—$1.50 a day for nine months to support six of them. It does not stand to reason that those children and he himself can have natural food and be naturally dressed. His children are often sick, and he has to call in doctors.

O'Donnell himself earned $133 a year. How, the committee asked, did he feed a family of four on that?

I got a couple of dollars worth of coal last winter, and the wood I picked up myself. I goes around with a shovel and picks up clams and food . . . We eat them. I don't get them to sell but just to eat for the family. That is the way my brother lives, mostly.

The committee learned from another witness that

workers almost invariably live in filthy tenement houses or in cellars or garrets . . . They are really uninhabitable. Swarms of children go about the street nearly naked; they come and go in that way and they are growing up to be the worst part of the community. They know no education.

Rents in the slums were $10 to $15 a month—a huge sum to be taken out of weekly earnings of $8 or less.

The workday in the 1880s was still dawn to dusk or close to that. The shorter-work-hours movement had brought about laws recognizing eight or 10 hours as a legal day's labor, but so big were their loopholes and so weakly were the laws enforced that they did little to cut the hours the American worker was "free" to toil.

No wonder, then, the movement for an eight-hour day saw a great revival in the mid-1880s. It got its impetus from the Federation of Organized Trades and Labor Unions, a body of national unions formed in 1881. More craft than mixed in nature, the Federation, in contrast to the Knights of Labor, grew slowly at first, hindered by the bad times of 1883 to 1885. In October of 1884, the Federation decided on an all-out campaign for the eight-hour day. It was slow going at first. A year later, the Federation of Organized Trades and Labor Unions set May 1, 1886, as the target. A national general strike would be called that day if the eight-hour day had not been granted to all workers.

Now the movement picked up speed. "There is eight-hour agitation everywhere," observed John Swinton early in 1886. The *New York Times* called the movement "un-American," and other papers warned it would bring about "lower wages, poverty and social degradation for the American worker."

But the workers did not listen. They flocked into the unions, singing:

> *We mean to make things over*
> > *We're tired of toil for nought*
> *But bare enough to live on; never*
> > *An hour for thought.*
> *We want to feel the sunshine: we*
> > *Want to smell the flowers*
> *We're sure that God has willed it*
> > *And we mean to have eight hours.*
> *We're summoning our forces from*
> > *Shipyard, shop and mill*
> *Eight hours for work, eight hours for rest*
> > *Eight hours for what we will!*

In the mining towns they sang:

> *We're brave and gallant miner boys who*
> > *work down underground*
> *For courage and good nature no finer can*
> > *be found*

We work both late and early, and get but
little pay
To support our wives and children in free
Amerikay.

If satan took the blacklegs, I'm sure 'twould
be no sin;
What peace and happiness 'twould be for
us poor working men.
Eight hours we'd have for working, eight
hours we'd have for play;
Eight hours we'd have for sleeping in free
Amerikay.

11

A BOMB AT HAYMARKET

May 1 came sunny and clear to Chicago.

It was Saturday, always a work day. But not this May 1 of 1886. Getting up that morning, workers put on their best clothes, took their wives and children, and walked toward Michigan Avenue where the parade was to start. They joked and laughed and sang on the way:

> Toiling millions now are waking
> See them marching on.
> All the tyrants now are shaking
> Ere their power's gone.

As the crowds surged into the broad avenue, they passed squads of armed police and state militia, standing by to enforce "law and order." Up on the rooftops the marchers could see Pinkerton detectives and more police squatting behind their rifles. Out of sight in the state armories the National Guard stood with Gatling guns, ready to march.

It was only a strike for shorter hours. But the employers acted as though it were revolution. With the help of the press, they could easily make it appear so. For several years now Chicago had been the center of radical movements. Socialists and anarchists had made the city their headquarters. There were not many in number, but some had risen to leadership in the local labor movement. Albert Parsons, a short, slim Southerner with jet-black hair and

76

flowing mustache, had arrived in Chicago in 1873 with his lovely Mexican-Indian wife, Lucy. In the depression of the seventies he had become a socialist and a popular labor organizer. Now 38, he was a leader of Chicago's Eight-Hour League, along with his best friend, 31-year-old August Spies, a German-born socialist.

As Parsons with his wife and two children joined the thousands massed on Michigan Avenue, Spies came running up with a copy of the Chicago *Mail*. The parade was about to begin. Parsons had only a minute to glance at the editorial Spies held out to him:

There are two dangerous ruffians at large in this city; two sneaking cowards who are trying to create trouble. One of them is named Parsons; the other is named Spies . . .

These two fellows have been at work fomenting disorder for the past ten years. They should have been driven out of the city long ago. They would not be tolerated in any other community on earth.

Parsons and Spies . . . have no love for the eight-hour movement . . . They are looking for riot and plunder . . .

Mark them for today. Keep them in view. Hold them personally responsible for any trouble that occurs. Make an example of them if trouble does occur.

Then the tide of workers rolled forward, and the Parsons family, holding hands, moved up into the front ranks. The demonstration was 80,000 strong. They marched, heads up, happy, feeling strong in the sure knowledge that hundreds of thousands of other workers were parading all over the country.

So May 1 in Chicago came and went—peacefully. Strikes took place in industrial centers everywhere. Some employers forestalled trouble by granting the shorter hours at the last minute. This affected 150,000 workers. About 190,000 others quit work, and 40,000 of these got their demands in whole or in part.

May 2 was Sunday. Again, a peaceful day.

May 3 began quietly enough. But that afternoon the Chicago police tangled with striking workers at the McCormick Harvester plant. As strikebreakers were leaving the shop gates, the strikers flung sticks and stones. Police rushed up with clubs and guns. Four workers were killed and several others wounded.

A meeting to protest police brutality was called by the labor unions for the next night in Haymarket Square. It was a long rectangle where Randolph Street ran east and west between Desplaines and Halsted. Big factories and warehouses walled in most of it.

Invited to speak, August Spies arrived at eight-thirty. He found only a small crowd there. But he climbed up on a wagon and began talking. Twenty minutes later word passed up from the crowd that Parsons had turned up. Spies got down, and Parsons began talking. He discussed labor's economic problems, then raised a warning:

There is nothing in the eight-hour movement to excite the capitalists. Do you know that the military are under arms, and a Gatling gun is ready to mow you down? Is this Germany or Russia or Spain? Whenever you make a demand for ... an increase in pay, the militia and the deputy sheriff and the Pinkerton men are called out and you are shot and clubbed and murdered in the streets. I am not here for the purpose of inciting anybody, but to speak out to tell the facts as they exist, even though it shall cost me my life before morning ... It behooves you, as you love your wife and children, if you don't want to see them perish with hunger, killed or cut down like dogs in the street, Americans, in the interest of your liberty and your independence, to arm, to arm yourselves.

Now it was 10 o'clock. Parsons had talked nearly an hour. He introduced another socialist, Samuel Fielden. "The law is your enemy," Fielden told the crowd, numbering about 1,200 by this hour. "We are rebels against it. The law is framed only for those who are your enslavers."

Only 10 minutes had gone when a chill wind swept in a curtain of rain. Many in the crowd ran for shelter, but Fielden kept on talking. Ten minutes more, and he was near his last sentence. "In conclusion," he said—and stopped dead. A long column of 180 police had suddenly appeared in the square. It marched directly to the wagon.

*A weekly newspaper's depiction of the dynamite
bomb exploding in Haymarket Square in Chicago on
May 4, 1886 as striking workers met to protest police
brutality.* (Courtesy New York Historical Society)

Fielden fell back a step, bewildered. The people, huddled together in the rain, wondered what was happening.

Headed by two captains, the police drew up at the tail of the wagon. "In the name of the people of the State of Illinois," said Captain Ward, "I command this meeting immediately and peaceably to disperse!"

Silence.

Again he shouted his order, this time adding, "And I call upon you and you [pointing to bystanders] to assist."

Fielden spoke up. "But captain, we are peaceable," he said. And with Spies and others standing on the wagon, he began to climb down.

Suddenly there was a glaring red flash and a terrific explosion. A dynamite bomb had come out of no one knew where and hit the ground near the front rank of the police. Seven police were fatally wounded and 67 others hurt. In the darkness the police opened fire on the crowd. People ran, screamed, cursed, moaned. Then the maddened police charged, clubbing and shooting. In a few seconds the square was red with blood. Ten workers fell dead, and another 50 were wounded.

The next day Chicago's press and the nation's screamed for revenge. The police invaded the working-class neighborhoods. "Make the raids and look up the law afterwards," said the state's attorney. It was instantly decided, without any proof, that the bomb was the work of anarchists, socialists, communists. The *New York Times* declared:

No disturbance of the peace that has occurred in the United States since the war of the rebellion has excited public sentiment through the Union as it is excited by the Anarchists' murder of policemen in Chicago on Tuesday night. We say murder with the fullest consciousness of what that word means. It is silly to speak of the crime as a riot. All the evidence goes to show that it was concerted, deliberately planned, and coolly executed murder . . . Cowardly savages who plotted and carried out this murder shall suffer the death they deserve.

The *Labor Enquirer* took another view:

Twice as many honest men may be murdered in a coal mine, as have been killed in Chicago, and there isn't any noise at all about it. The American press is a wonderfully lopsided affair.

But that editorial comment was an exception. "There are no good anarchists except dead anarchists," the St. Louis Globe-Democrat said. The Columbus, Ohio Journal noted, "There are too many unhung anarchists and rebels." The Philadelphia Press urged, "Give the bullet to the disorderly agitators." The Washington Post announced the anarchists were "a horde of foreigners, representing almost the lowest stratum found in humanity's formation."

Harper's Weekly demanded "the most complete and summary methods of repression." The New York *Tribune* called for "only the sharpest and sternest application of force . . . The anarchists are not honest workingmen, but pirates . . . and as such they must be dealt with." Agreeing with the *Tribune*, the New York *Sun* proposed deporting every confessed anarchist and restricting immigration to keep out "foreign savages, with their dynamite bombs and anarchic purposes."

Who threw that bomb is still a mystery. But the police had no doubts. The anarchists must be guilty. Eight men—Parsons, Spies, Fielden, Fischer, Schwab, Neebe, Lingg and Engel—were picked up and tried for conspiracy to murder. No proof was offered that any of the eight had planted or thrown a bomb. Only three of the men were actually at the meeting. Nor was it proved that the speakers had incited to violence. Chicago's own mayor said that the speeches were "tame."

As everyone expected, the eight were convicted. On the day they were to be sentenced, one of the accused, August Spies, said to the court:

If you think by hanging us you can stamp out the labor movement . . . the movement from which the downtrodden millions, the millions who toil in want and misery expect salvation—if this is your opinion, then hang us! Here you will tread upon a spark, but there and there, behind you

*and in front of you, and everywhere, flames blaze up. It is
a subterranean fire. You cannot put it out . . .*

*If you would once more have people suffer the penalty of
death because they have dared to tell the truth . . . then I
will proudly and defiantly pay the costly price! Call your
hangman! . . . Truth crucified in Socrates, in Christ, in
Giordano Bruno, in Huss, in Galileo still lives—they and
others whose number is legion have preceded us on this
path. We are ready to follow.*

Lyman Trumbull, long a Senator from Illinois, said that
he was not satisfied with the manner in which the trial
was conducted:

*It took place at a time of great public excitement, when
it was about impossible that they should have a fair and
impartial trial. A terrible crime has been committed which
was attributed to the anarchists, and in some respects the
trial had the appearance of a trial of an organization
known as anarchists, rather than of persons indicted for
murder.*

Seven of the men were condemned to death.
One of America's leading novelists, William Dean Howells, said:

*I have never believed them guilty of murder, or of any-
thing but their opinions, and I do not think they were justly
convicted. This case constitutes the greatest wrong that
ever threatened our fame as a nation.*

The voices of dissent, at first few in number, grew stronger
and louder. One liberal, Henry Demarest Lloyd, wrote:

*I have always had a great doubt as to whether the bomb
was thrown by an anarchist at all; as to whether it was not
thrown by a police minion for the purpose of breaking up
the eight-hour movement.*

It took great courage to speak up for the condemned men.
The press whipped the public into a state of hysterical fear

of radicals. And when the Supreme Court refused to grant a writ of error, the injustice was cloaked in legality.

Lucy Parsons would not give up the fight for her husband's and the other men's lives. She talked to people on street corners day after day to plead their cause. On one day alone on the streets of Chicago she sold 5,000 copies at 5 cents each of a pamphlet called *Was It a Fair Trial: An Appeal to the Governor of Illinois.*

But Governor Oglesby refused to interfere with the court's sentence.

On November 11, 1887, Spies, Parsons, Fisher and Engel were taken from their cells, their arms tied, their wrists handcuffed and their bodies draped in white muslin shrouds. They were marched to the scaffold where they quietly took their places on the trap. Hoods were put over their heads, and the nooses slipped around their necks.

The 200 witnesses were seated in frozen silence on benches before the scaffold. Suddenly, from under Spies's hood came his voice:

There will come a time when our silence will be more powerful than the voices you strangle today!

And Parson's voice rang out:

Will I be allowed to speak, O men of America? Let me speak, Sheriff Matson! Let the voice of the people be heard!

And the trap was sprung.

But the Haymarket case was not yet ended. Four men were executed, and one had killed himself in his cell; but three others were still in prison. The movement to get them out was soon underway.

In the next years each governor of Illinois was petitioned to release the Haymarket prisoners. All were deaf to the pleas. Then, in 1892, a man named John Peter Altgeld was elected governor.

Like Lincoln, Altgeld started from the humblest beginnings. His mother and father were poor farmers who emigrated to America when their boy was three months old. All the schooling John had added up to less than a year. At 16 he served in the Union Army. Not long after the Civil War, he made friends with a lawyer, studied law with him and opened his own office. Like many lawyers, he soon got into politics and began making a lot of money in real estate. But he always stayed honest, rigidly honest in that gilded age when corruption in both business and politics was almost standard practice.

Soon after Altgeld's inauguration, a petition for pardon of the Haymarket prisoners carrying over 60,000 signatures was presented to the new governor. He had kept silent on the case while his political star rose. Now he took the records and began studying them.

"If you go through that record," one advisor told him, "you will see that you ought to pardon all three of them and I hope you will. If you do, though, it will be the end of your political career."

"If I decide they were innocent," Altgeld replied, "I will pardon them, by God, no matter what happens to my career."

It was a lonely time for Altgeld. He had to face not only only the facts themselves but what they might mean for his own strong ambition to be senator. Through the spring of 1893 he kept reading the record and writing down his thoughts about it. On June 26, he acted. He signed pardons for the three men in the Joliet prison and released his pardon message to the press.

"The storm will break now," his secretary said. "Yes," the governor replied, "I was prepared for that. It was merely doing right."

The storm did break, and it was wild, terrible, unrelenting. For the governor had not pardoned the men because they had already served seven years in prison, or because it was an act of mercy to do so. No, he pardoned them because he was convinced by the evidence that the three in prison and the five who were dead were all innocent. As to who did throw the bomb, Altgeld said:

It is shown here that the bomb was, in all probability, thrown by someone seeking personal revenge; that a course had been pursued by the authorities which would naturally cause this; that for a number of years prior to the

*Haymarket affair there had been labor troubles, and in
several cases a number of laboring people, guilty of no
offense, had been shot down in cold blood by Pinkerton
men, and none of the murderers were brought to justice.
The evidence taken at coroners' inquests and presented
here, shows that in at least two cases men were fired on and
killed when they were running away, and there was conse-
quently no occasion to shoot, yet nobody was punished; that
in Chicago there had been a number of strikes in which
some of the police not only took sides against the men, but
without any authority of law invaded and broke up peaceable meetings, and in scores of cases brutally clubbed
people who were guilty of no offense whatsoever.*

And what of the witnesses and testimony produced by
the state against the defendants? Again Altgeld:

*It is further shown here that much of the evidence given
at the trial was a pure fabrication; that some of the prominent police officials, in their zeal, not only terrorized
ignorant men by throwing them into prison and threaten-
ing them with torture if they refused to swear anything
desired, but that they offered money and employment to
those who would consent to do this. Further, that they
deliberately planned to have fictitious conspiracies formed
in order that they might get the glory of discovering them.
In addition to the evidence in the record of some witnesses
who swore that they had been paid small sums of money,
etc., several documents are here referred to.*

Altgeld's message showed that the jury had not been
chosen by chance, as the law required, but by a bailiff who
said, "Those fellows are going to be hanged as certain as
death." And finally, Altgeld made plain the ferocious bias
of presiding Judge Gary against the defendants.

The newspapers gave little space to the substance of
Altgeld's message. Instead, they turned the public's mind
away from the meaning of the message by violent personal
attacks upon its author. He was called everything from "a
wild- haired demagogue" to "the Nero of the last decade of
the 19th century." The Toledo *Blade*'s comment was typi-

cal: "Governor Altgeld has encouraged anarchy, rapine and the overthrow of civilization." Overnight Altgeld became the most hated man in America.

Why? Because he was telling the working class that its leaders were being convicted in the courts on framed evidence. To Altgeld, the betrayal of democracy and justice in the Haymarket trial was a greater menace to America than anything the defendants had ever thought or done.

12

WHICH WAY:
GOMPERS OR DEBS?

1 886—the year of labor's "great uprising"—had come and gone. But, as a Massachusetts labor paper noted, "The wage system remained, the factory whistle blew early in the morning, the machine and its tender ran all the day, the envelope was scantily filled on Saturday night."

The "uprising" had collapsed. Haymarket was its end. By the close of the year, only 15,000 workers retained the gains they had made through the shorter-hour movement. The Knights of Labor shrank as quickly as they had expanded.

In place of the uplift unionism of the Knights came a new kind of trade unionism. Led by skilled workers, the American Federation of Labor took a completely different tack. Two of the founders of the American Federation of Labor in 1886 were Samuel Gompers and Adolph Strasser of the Cigar Makers Union. As Strasser told a Senate committee:

We have no ultimate ends. We are going on from day to day. We are fighting only for immediate objects—objects that can be realized in a few years.

He did not mean the American Federation of Labor leaders were unaware of the bloody battle going on between labor and capital. The Federation's constitution recognized it:

A struggle is going on in the nations of the world between capital and labor which must grow in intensity from year to year and work disastrous results to the toiling millions of all nations if not combined for mutual protection and benefit.

But neither did the American Federation of Labor mean to change the system.

Its goal was "a fair day's wage for a fair day's work."

Its method was to form unions for each of the skilled crafts.

Its ideas came mostly from Gompers, the man who headed the American Federation of Labor for 37 years. He was a heavyset, strong-jawed man with a thick mop of hair and rimless glasses. He had learned about trade unionism very early. He was born of Dutch-Jewish parents in London. He father was active in the British cigar makers' union. Coming to America at 13, young Gompers had lived on the East Side of New York, knowing poverty and struggle and absorbing socialist ideas from European radicals he worked with in the cigar-making shops. He was stirred deeply by their goals in his youth, but later saw how impractical many of their theories were and turned against them.

He wanted to build a practical American labor movement, with bread-and-butter goals. And the way to do it, as he often said, was to make the American Federation of Labor "the business organization of the workers."

Gompers' way got results for the limited group of *skilled* workers he sought to reach. Workers of the same craft were organized into national trade unions, with each taking care of its own problems. The Federation did not try to control its affiliates' affairs. It let them be independent, offering them a center for cooperation only when they asked for it.

Gompers knew unions had to be strong to match the power of the corporations, so high dues and initiation fees were charged. This made it possible to hire full-time union officials to carry on the work of organizing, negotiating contracts, running meetings, keeping records, conducting strikes.

The businesslike approach helped the American Federation of Labor build solid unions. They won higher pay, shorter hours and better working conditions. Their policy was peaceful bargaining wherever possible, strikes only where negotiations failed. The test that all other unions had failed before—the ability to survive depressions—the American Federation of Labor passed.

By 1890 the Federation was the central force in American labor. In the next 25 years in the unionized industries it helped raise average weekly wages from $17.57 to $23.98 and cut the average working week from 54.4 to 48.9 hours.

Unorganized labor benefited too during the same period, for their weekly earnings rose from $8.82 to $11.52, and the working week dropped from 62.2 to 55.6 hours.

So the American Federation of Labor earned its success. But it did not look ahead to what was already in sight. The mass production industries were breaking down more and more of the old crafts and creating many million more unskilled jobs. The gulf separating wage earner and employer yawned wider. One worker put it this way:

The employer has pretty much the same feeling toward the men that he has toward his machinery. He wants to get as much as he can out of his men at the cheapest rate . . . That is all he cares for generally.

President Cleveland saw what was happening. In his 1888 message to Congress he said:

As we view the achievements of aggregated capital, we discover the existence of trusts, combinations and monopolies, while the citizen is struggling far in the rear or is trampled to death beneath an iron heel. Corporations, which should be the carefully restrained creatures of the law and the servants of the people, are fast becoming the people's masters.

Nothing stood in the way of Mellon, Morgan, Rockefeller, Frick, Carnegie and the scores of others building industrial empires. Their mines, mills and railroads employed tens of thousands of workers, and the great mass of them were unskilled. At that same moment the American Federation of Labor was building unions of craftsmen, ignoring the millions of unskilled and unorganized.

It was a policy that could lead to disaster.

Governor Altgeld of Illinois understood that. He had long been sympathetic with the workingman, and he tried to point out a path for him to follow:

This is an age of concentration. Everywhere there is concentration and combination of capital and of those factors which today rule the world . . . The world gives only when it is obliged to, and respects only those who compel its respect . . . Let all men of America who toil with their hands once stand together and no more complaints will be heard about unfair treatment.

There was one labor leader who had learned that lesson the hard way. He was Eugene Victor Debs, born in Terre Haute, Indiana. At 14 he was working in the town's railroad yards. By 25 he was an officer of the Brotherhood of Locomotive Firemen.

For 13 years Debs fought to build his craft union. But the success and popularity he earned did not blind him to the fact that craft unions had outlived their usefulness. He said:

A modern industrial plant has a hundred trades and parts of trades represented in its working force. To have these workers parcelled out to a hundred unions is to divide and not to organize them, to give them over to factions and petty leadership and leave them an easy prey to the machinations of the enemy. The dominant craft should control the plant or, rather, the union, and it should embrace the entire working force. This is the industrial plan, the modern method applied to modern conditions, and it will in time prevail.

Eugene V. Debs, who thought labor could match the
power of the new mass industries only if all the work-
ers, skilled and unskilled, were united in one organi-
zation. (Courtesy New York University Tamiment
Library)

Debs saw how rivalries and jealousies among the railroad brotherhoods made it easy for the corporations to get their way with each separately. And besides, only 90,000 workers, a small fraction of all the railwaymen, were in the brotherhoods. The great mass of unskilled and semiskilled had never been organized.

Debs made the break with craft unionism when the Switchmen's Union struck in 1893 and the brotherhoods refused to support the workers. Disgusted, he resigned his union post and moved to form a new organization, an industrial union.

Debs was now 38, a lean, muscular six-footer. His bald dome and jutting chin were known almost everywhere the rails went. Self-taught, he was a man with great charm and eloquence. From the age of 19 he gave all his strength to the cause of labor.

My grip was always packed, [he wrote] to tramp through a railroad yard in the rain, snow or sleet half the night. To be ordered out of the roundhouse for being an agitator or to be put off a train, were all in the program.

Debs's new organization, the American Railway Union, was born in Chicago in June 1893. Its aim was to unite all railroad workers into one industrial union, instead of dividing them into separate crafts. But there was one great exception—you had to be white. The new union's constitution shut out blacks. Debs knew it was a tragic mistake; he led a strong convention fight to admit blacks but lost by a close margin. Later he charged that those who had worked to keep blacks out had been "traitors to the union, sent to the convention at the instigation of the corporations to defeat the unity of the working class."

Into the new union rushed railroadmen by the thousands. In five months charters were issued to 87 lodges. By year's end a dozen of the major and minor roads were solidly organized. Most of those who joined were the unskilled and semiskilled—who had not been eligible for the brotherhoods—but there were many firemen and engineers, too.

The American Railway Union's first test came with a strike on James J. Hill's Great Northern Railroad. It began in April 1894, after the men had taken three pay cuts. The average wage on the line was $40 a month. From the beginning the strike was solid. Despite Hill's threats of mass firings and a federal warning that any interference with the train-borne mail would be punished by two years in prison and a $10,000 fine, under Debs's leadership the 9,000 employees refused to return to work. In 18 days the road caved in and accepted arbitration. The union won 97½% of its demands—a total pay raise of $146,000 a month.

That June the jubilant railway workers met in their first national convention at Chicago. They had reason to celebrate. Their fledgling industrial union had just licked tough Jim Hill, and now 150,000 men had joined up. They roared out support of President Debs when he told them that if the workers would only "march together, vote together and fight together," they would soon enjoy all their rights.

In those early years of the 1890s, two men towered over labor—Gompers and Debs. Each was taking his own path in leadership. Gompers believed in *craft* unionism, in organizing workers according to their special skills or distinct occupations. Debs thought labor's future in an era of mass industries lay in organizing *all* workers, skilled or unskilled, who worked in the same industry.

Both men's ideas were soon to be tested in tremendous struggles with two giants of industry.

13

THE BATTLE
OF HOMESTEAD

It was three o'clock in the morning when the two big barges slipped into the mouth of the Monongahela River. Through the thick fog the men crowded on the decks could barely see the lights of Pittsburgh gleaming from the shore. Uniforms were handed out and the men put them on. They wore the standard Pinkerton outfit: slouch hat, metal-buttoned blouse, dark blue pants with light stripes down the sides. Some of the men sat on the crates packed with the rifles, pistols and ammunition. The others lay on the decks or stood at the rail, discussing the secret mission in tense whispers.

There were over 300 of them, picked up by recruiting agents in Chicago and New York. Most were jobless, some were criminals on the run, others Civil War veterans or ex-policemen, the rest the men running the show—experienced professionals of the Pinkerton National Detective Agency. For the past 40 years Pinkertons had been used by industrialists whenever there were strikes to be broken or unions to be smashed. By now the agency had 2,000 trained men and 30,000 reserves.

This July night of 1892, the Pinkertons were in the pay of the Carnegie Steel Company. They were sneaking up the river in darkness, hoping to make a surprise landing at Homestead, where Carnegie had shut down one of his giant steel mills in an effort to break the workers' union. In return, the workers had thrown a picket line around the plant to keep out scabs and stop production.

Two forces were about to collide while the whole country watched.

One one side stood Andrew Carnegie. The poor immigrant boy had arrived in America at 13. By the time he was 40 "the little Scotch pirate," as the men on Wall Street called him, had beaten off the other tigers in the economic jungle and made himself master of American iron and steel production. In the 1880s his dozen plants around Pittsburgh were filling his private pockets with untaxed profits of $2 to $20 million a year.

On the other side stood America's most powerful craft union, the Amalgamated Association of Iron and Steel Workers. It was the pride of Sam Gompers and his American Federation of Labor. Nationally the union had 24,000 members. Here at Homestead it had 800, only one-fifth of the 3,800 workers the plant employed. The great majority of these workers were unskilled, and many of them recent arrivals from eastern Europe—Slavs, Hungarians, Rumanians. The union had turned its back on them, as it had on most of the immigrants and the unskilled. It was a craft union, concerned only with the skilled workers, who were in the minority.

The skilled union men at the plant worked an eight-hour day, earning at peak production maximums ranging from $35 to $70 a week, while the semiskilled averaged $25 a week. At the other end were the 3,000 unskilled day laborers at 14 cents per hour, a little under $10 a week. They worked 12 hours daily, most of them, and every day of the year except Christmas and the Fourth of July. Nonunion, all.

How did the unskilled workers and their families live on such wages? A social researcher, Margaret F. Byington, studied Homestead and reported:

A man who has a family of normal size to support, can provide for them only a two-room tenement in a crowded court, with no sanitary conveniences; a supply of food below the minimum sufficient for mere physical well-being; in-

surance that makes provision which is utterly inadequate for the family left without a breadwinner; a meager expenditure for clothes and furniture, and an almost negligible margin for recreation, education and savings.

Many can, to be sure, add to their earnings by working seven days a week, instead of six; by working twelve hours a day instead of ten; but after all we are talking of standards of life and labor for an American industry, and common sense will scarcely sanction such a week of work. Many too, as we have seen, take in lodgers, but do it at the cost of decency and health.

And Homestead itself, what was it like to live in? Hamlin Garland, the journalist, took a look:

The streets were horrible; the buildings were poor; the sidewalks were sunken and full of holes; and the crossings were formed of sharp-edged stones like rocks in a river bed. Everywhere the yellow mud of streets lay kneaded into sickly masses, through which groups of pale, lean men slouched in faded garments, grimy with the soot and dirt of the mills. The town was as squalid as could well be imagined, and the people were mainly of the discouraged and sullen type to be found everywhere where labor passed into the brutalizing stage of severity.

Inside the plant, said one visitor, you saw:

Everywhere in the enormous sheds were pits gaping like the mouth of hell, and ovens emitting a terrible degree of heat, with grimy men filling and lining them. One man jumps down, works desperately for a few minutes, and is then pulled up, exhausted. Another immediately takes his place; there is no hesitation.

The accident rate under these conditions was enormous. Total deaths in the year 1891 were around 300 in Pittsburgh's steel mills, and the injured men numbered over 2,000. Men suffered and died from explosions, burnings, asphyxiation, electric shocks, falls, crushing and a dozen other causes.

There was reason enough, then, for the men to organize and seek better wages and conditions. In 1889 the Amalgamated Association of Iron and Steel Workers had won a three-year contract from Carnegie. Now, as the agreement was about to end, the union asked for negotiations to renew it. In charge at Homestead was Henry Clay Frick, fresh from a career of union busting in the coke fields.

The workers knew Frick's preference: He would like to break the union. But what about Carnegie? He had recently written in the *Forum* magazine:

The right of the workingman to combine and to form trades-unions is no less sacred than the right of the manufacturer to enter into associations and conferences with his fellows . . . My experience has been that trades-unions upon the whole are beneficial both to labor and to capital.

Carnegie had dealt with the union once because it made wages uniform throughout the industry and took away any advantage competitors might have had in lower wages. But now he had driven his competitors out of the market. His steel trust no longer needed the union.

While he went on talking pro-union, he wrote out a policy statement for Frick that said:

There has been forced upon this Firm the question whether its Works are to be run "Union" or "Non-Union." As the vast majority of our employees are Non-Union, the Firm has decided that the minority must give place to the majority. These workers, therefore, will be necessarily Non-Union after the expiration of the present agreement . . . This action is not taken in any spirit of hostility to labor organizations, but every man will see that the firm cannot run Union and Non-Union. It must be one or the other.

Then Carnegie sailed for his annual long vacation in Scotland, and left Frick to get rid of the union.

Negotiations began in February 1892. Steel prices were booming, and the union asked for a raise. Frick's reply was to propose a wage cut. Negotiations dragged on. Frick began building a high fence around the mill, cutting rifle

slits in it and topping it with barbed wire. The steelworkers dubbed the plant Fort Frick and concluded the company meant to smash the union. Then Frick gave the men
an ultimatum—settle on his terms in one month or the
company would stop dealing with the union.

Angered, the men carried out a mock public hanging of
Frick. With this as an excuse, he shut down the mill and
locked out the workers two days before the contract was
to end.

At a mass meeting, the 3,000 unskilled workers—despite the fact they had long been shunned by the union—
voted to stand solid with the 800 Amalgamated men. Frick
moved fast to bring in scabs. Earlier he had secretly hired
Pinkerton men to study the grounds. Now he ordered 300
Pinkerton guards to get through the picket line and take
over the plant so that they could protect the scabs he
wanted to hire.

The mood of the Homestead workers was voiced by John
Fitch, a special investigator, in a report of the situation:

The Homestead men had been working in the mill at that
place, many of them since it was first built. They had seen
it grow from a small beginning to one of the finest and best
equipped plants in the world. They were proud of that plant
and proud of the part that they had had in its progress.

Over the hills rising from the river were their cottages,
many of them owned by the workingmen . . . and now these
homes were in jeopardy. They could have gone back to work
. . . But that meant giving up their union . . . self-disenfran-
chisement. So when the Pinkerton men came, the Home-
stead steel workers saw in their approach an attempt at
subjugation at the hands of an armed force of unauthorized
individuals. A mob of men with guns coming to take their
jobs . . . to take away the chance to work, to break up their
homes—that is what passed through the minds of the
Homestead men that morning.

At four o'clock on the morning of July 6, 1892, a workers'
patrol sighted the Pinkerton barges a mile below Homestead. Whistles screamed through the town and ten thousand men, women and children rushed down to the

riverbank. The barges hit the beach at dawn. All along the river's edge the Pinkertons saw carbines, rifles, shotguns, pistols, revolvers, clubs and stones in the hands of the workers. Wildly excited voices shouted to the Pinkertons to turn back. Some in the crowd thought one barge carried strikebreakers and the other Pinkerton guards.

An advance group of Pinkertons stepped forward with their Winchester repeaters. The gangplank went down, and they started to cross it to shore. A striker lay down upon it, barring the way with his body. As a Pinkerton tried to kick him aside, the striker pulled out a revolver and shot him in the thigh.

Firing began at once from both sides. The Pinkertons on the gangplank blasted into the crowd, shooting down several workers. From topside on the barges, rifle fire cut down 30 Homestead men at once, while from the bank the crowd kept up fire on the barges.

The battle was to go on for 13 hours, the guards shooting over the water and the workers from behind barricades of scrap metal they quickly threw up.

It was one of the bloodiest battles in American labor history. The final count was never certain, but it is estimated that some 20 Pinkerton men and 40 strikers were shot. Seven Pinkertons and nine strikers died. At five in the afternoon, the Pinkertons put up a white flag and marched unarmed up the shore where they were beaten badly by the enraged wives of the workers before the sheriff's men took over.

The next day the company told the press:

This outbreak settles one matter forever, and that is that the Homestead mill hereafter will never again recognize the Amalgamated Association nor any other labor organization.

But the workers were not scared. They were optimistic. They had won the first battle. They settled down to finish the war. Their only worry was the possible use of the state militia against them.

News of bloody Homestead shook the outside world. Unions sent messages of support to the locked-out men. In

Pittsburgh one union insisted the city council give back
Carnegie's gift of a million dollars for a free library because, they said, the money was tainted with workers'
blood.

The chairman of a Congressional investigating committee criticized the union's effort to keep nonunion men from
scabbing. He said:

*The right of any man to labor, upon whatever terms he
and his employer agree, whether he belong to a labor
organization or not, and the right of a person or corporation
(which in law is also a person) to employ any one to labor
in a lawful business is secured by the laws of the land.*

But Andrew Carnegie himself, back in 1886, had said:

*To expect that one dependent upon his daily wage for the
necessaries of life will stand by peaceably and see a new
man employed in his stead is to expect much. This poor
man may have a wife and children dependent upon his
labor . . . There is an unwritten law among the best
workmen: "Thou shalt not take thy neighbor's job."*

The steel master's workmen had already learned the
bitter lesson that what Mr. Carnegie said as a humanitar-
ian in public was not what Mr. Carnegie the businessman
did in private.

The Homestead workers did not relax their guard. They
took care of their wounded and watched for another invasion of Pinkertons. A few days later, not Pinkertons but
8,000 members of the Pennsylvania National Guard suddenly took over the town, pitching camp on a hill overlook-
ing it. Their aim, the commanding general said, was "to
restore law and order."

But they stayed for over three months, while the company brought in scab after scab until nearly 2,000 were
inside, operating the steel mill. It seemed incredible that
the locked-out men had held firm for almost five months.
But finally, the troops, the scabs, costly court actions,
evictions from company houses, press attacks, hunger
became too much. The feeling grew they were doomed to

lose. Men began drifting away, hunting for other jobs. The unskilled workers, whose jobs could more easily be filled by scabs, voted to go back to work. Their loyalty had been heroic, for the union had never offered to take them in.

A few days later the union members, too, voted to return to the mill. The Homestead strike was broken.

Frick cabled Carnegie:

OUR VICTORY IS NOW COMPLETE AND MOST GRATIFYING. DO NOT THINK WE WILL EVER HAVE SERIOUS LABOR TROUBLE AGAIN. WE HAD TO TEACH OUR EMPLOYEES A LESSON AND WE HAVE TAUGHT THEM ONE THEY WILL NEVER FORGET.

Carnegie replied to Frick:

LIFE WORTH LIVING AGAIN. CONGRATULATE ALL AROUND.

The defeat crushed the union in Homestead. Frick himself was on hand to watch the Amalgamated men ask for their old jobs. Almost none got them back. They who had once been the cream of the plant—the skilled, the indispensable—saw their jobs filled by new men, swiftly trained to take the craftsmen's place. Mechanization of the mills made it easy—skill didn't count so much.

The industrywide blacklist kept the union men out of every steel mill. It was a great blow to the Amalgamated Association of Iron and Steel Workers and the American Federation of Labor. In two years the Amalgamated lost half of its national membership as one employer after another refused to deal with it any more. By 1910 it had only one contract with a small company. Not until the 1930s would another union rise to lift the workers out of poverty and fear.

At Homestead, the defeat of the 1892 strike meant a 12-hour day and a seven-day week for almost all the workers. Pinkerton spies were installed everywhere. Wages were slashed far more than the beaten men had expected. Grievance committees were done away with. Workers meetings were banned. Living and working conditions sank so low a British visitor a few years after the strike called it "a veritable Hell of a place."

As for Mr. Carnegie, he wired a friend in 1899, "Ashamed to tell you profits these days. Prodigious!" In 1900 the company's net was $40 million.

Out of Homestead came one of labor's best-known songs, called "Father Was Killed by the Pinkerton Men."

> 'Twas in a Pennsylvania town not very long ago
> Men struck against reduction of their pay
> Their millionaire employer with philanthropic show
> Had closed the work till starved they would obey
> They fought for home and right to live where they had
>   toiled so long
> But ere the sun had set some were laid low
> There're hearts now sadly grieving by that sad and bitter
>   wrong, God help them for it was a cruel blow.

CHORUS

> God help them tonight in their hour of affliction
> Praying for him whom they'll ne'er see again
> Hear the poor orphans tell their sad story
> "Father was killed by the Pinkerton men."
> Ye prating politicians, who boast protection creed,
> Go to Homestead and stop the orphans' cry,
> Protection for the rich man ye pander to his greed,
> His workmen they are cattle and may die.
> The freedom of the city in Scotland far away
> 'Tis presented to the millionaire suave,
> But here in Free America with protection in full sway
> His workmen get the freedom of the grave.

CHORUS

14

A MODEL TOWN GOES ON STRIKE

Homestead—the strike that tested craft unionism against a big steel corporation—happened in 1892.

Two years later another union—this time industrial, not craft—took on another corporation giant.

Would the industrial union do any better than Sam Gompers's defeated steelworkers?

The trouble began in Pullman, a suburb of Chicago named for George W. Pullman, the manufacturer of the sleeping car. Here lived 5,000 workers employed in Pullman's factories, who with their families made up the town's 12,000 residents.

The men made and repaired Pullman's dining, sleeping and club cars, which were operated under contract on 125,000 miles of railroad, some three-fourths of the nation's total trackage.

Founded in 1880, the town was Pullman's idea of a workers' utopia. A company pamphlet described it as

bordered with bright beds of flowers and green velvety stretches of lawn, shaded with trees, and dotted with parks and pretty water vistas, and glimpses here and there of artistic sweeps of landscape gardening.

The plant, the homes, and the public buildings and shops stood on a 300-acre site. There were 1,800 tenements for the workers, most of them brick, the rest frame. As the Pullman historian, Almont Lindsey, described the town:

> *Wide divergence existed in the character of Pullman homes. The brickyard dwellings, which George Pullman denied were a part of the town, consisted of small shanties without modern sewage facilities or other conveniences. In the most eastern part of Pullman, on Fulton Street, were located the great tenement blocks with a total of ten large buildings. Three stories tall and containing flats of two to four rooms, these buildings each accommodated from twelve to forty-eight families. Although modern, some of the facilities in these tenements were restricted: only one water faucet for each group of five families, and the same toilet for two or more families.*
> *In sharp contrast to the Fulton Street flats were the spacious nine-room cottages in the vicinity of the Florence Hotel. Designed for highly salaried Pullman officials, they were steam heated and equipped with a large fireplace, a bathroom, numerous closets, a laundry, and large bay windows. The rooms were commodious and artistically decorated.*

It is a model town, said the company pamphlet,

> *where all that is ugly and discordant and demoralizing is eliminated, and all that inspires to self-respect is generously provided.*

But was what really "inspires to self-respect"—independence, democracy, self-government—present in Pullman?

All the town officials were appointed by the Pullman Corporation. The *Pullman Journal* backed all the corporation's policies. Labor organizers and radical speakers were refused the rental or use of the public halls. A spy system ferreted out any sign or word critical of the authorities.

So obvious was Pullman's tight control of the town, the New York *Sun* in 1885 reported:

> *The people of Pullman are not happy and grumble at their situation even more than the inhabitants of towns not*

model are accustomed to do. They say that all this perfection of order costs them too much in money and imposes upon them an intolerable constraint . . . They want to run the municipal government themselves, according to the ordinary American fashion. They secretly rebel because the Pullman Company continues its watch and authority over them after working hours. They declare they are bound hand and foot by a philanthropic monopoly.

The company dominated every aspect of its workers' lives. It owned everything in the town—land, plant, houses, tenements, hotel, stores, bank, school, library, church, water and gas systems. As employer, George Pullman determined wages, as landlord he fixed rents, as banker he collected the savings.

Pullman knew how to make his business highly profitable. And he ran his town to be profitable too. He got water from Chicago for 4 cents, but charged his workers 10 cents. And the gas he paid 33 cents for, he priced at $2.25. No wonder one Pullman worker said:

We are born in a Pullman house, fed from the Pullman shop, taught in the Pullman school, catechized in the Pullman church, and when we die we shall be buried in the Pullman cemetery and go to the Pullman hell.

Pullman business was good business, even into the depression that began in 1893. During all its 26 years the company had paid its stockholders an annual dividend of 8%. And now, despite the national misery, the company not only paid the usual dividend but piled on top of it a surplus of over $4 million.

The profits grew fat, but not the workers. Reverend W. H. Carwardine, pastor of Pullman's church, reported:

After deducting rent the men invariably had only from one to six dollars or so on which to live for two weeks. One man has a pay check in his possession of two cents after paying rent. He has never cashed it, preferring to keep it as a memento. He has it framed. Another I saw the other day, for seven cents. The man had worked as a skilled mechanic

at ten hours a day for twelve days, and earned $9.07. He
keeps a widowed mother, and pays the rent, the house being
in his name. His half month's rent amounted to $9.00. The
seven cents was his, but he never claimed it.

When the depression came on, Pullman chopped wages
25 to 40%. Rents and prices in the model town, however,
he kept the same. Sinking deeper and deeper into debt
during the depression's first bitter winter, the workers felt
they had taken all they could. Debs's new American Railway Union encouraged them. They could join it because
the fact that Pullman ran a small railroad made them
eligible. To avoid company spies, they organized secretly
in nearby towns. In May 1894, they sent a committee to
the company to ask that the wage cuts be restored. The
company pleaded poverty. It added it was only keeping the
plant going in order to give the men work.

Reluctantly, the men went back to work, assured first
that the company would not fire any of the committee. But
the next day three of them were laid off. It was the spark
that exploded the pent-up rage of years of humiliation. The
men called a strike at once. Nearly 4,000 of them had
joined the American Railway Union, and they looked to
Debs for help. He had advised them earlier to go slow,
because he knew better than anyone how young and weak
and inexperienced the new union was.

Pullman promptly shut down the whole plant. His policy was to wait out the workers until starvation drove
them back. In a few weeks their families were suffering
terribly. When the American Railway Union opened its
convention in Chicago a month after the strike had begun,
the Pullman workers took their plight to the delegates:

We struck at Pullman because we were without hope. We
joined the American Railway Union because it gave us a
glimmer of hope . . .
Pullman, both the man and the town, is an ulcer on the
body politic. He owns the houses, the schoolhouses, and
churches of God in the town he gave his once humble name.
The revenue he derives from these, the wages he pays out
with one hand—the Pullman Palace Car Company, he

*takes back with the other—the Pullman Land Association.
He is able by this to bid under any contract car shop in this
country. His competitors in business, to meet this, must
reduce the wages of their men. This gives him the excuse to
reduce ours to conform to the market. His business rivals
must in turn scale down; so must he. And thus the merry
war—the dance of skeletons bathed in human tears—goes
on, and it will go on, brothers, forever, unless you, the
American Railway Union, stop it; end it; crush it out . . .*

*We will make you proud of us, brothers, if you will give
us the hand we need. Help us make our country better and
more wholesome . . . Teach arrogant grinders of the faces
of the poor that there still is a God of Israel, and if need be,
a Jehovah—a God of battles.*

Debs tried again and again to get arbitration of the
dispute. The company would not listen. From the floor
came a proposal that the American Railway Union boycott
Pullman cars, refusing to handle them anywhere in the
country until the company agreed to negotiate. Debs said
wait, let's try for arbitration once more. A committee of
strikers went to the company. Again Pullman said, "There
is nothing to arbitrate." The American Railway Union
then voted unanimously for a boycott to begin on June 26.

On that day the switchmen detached Pullman cars from
the trains. At once the men were fired. Then the other
members of the American Railway Union walked off the
job in protest. The boycott had become a strike. By the
second day 40,000 men had quit; two days later 125,000
were out and 20 railroads were tied up. Soon nearly every
train in the country was dead on its tracks.

It was the most effective strike on this scale the country
had ever seen. But Debs knew this was still a rookie union
pitted against veteran union busters. For even before the
boycott had begun, his industrial union was facing a far
stronger force than Pullman. It was the General Managers
Association, a semisecret organization representing 24 of
the nation's biggest railroads centering on Chicago. They
were a kind of industrial union of the railroad corporations, as the American Railway Union was of the railroad
workers. Now they stepped in to help Pullman.

The roads knew the boycott was not aimed at them; it was aimed at Pullman. But they saw in the boycott a chance to destroy the new industrial union movement before it could take hold of American labor. As the boycott was about to begin, the Association's chairman said, "We can handle the railway brotherhoods, but we cannot handle the American Railway Union . . . We cannot handle Debs. We have got to wipe him out."

So the Association took charge. Out of years of experience with strikes, Debs knew that if the union was to win, it had to keep the strike peaceful. He sent telegrams all over advising the unionists to stop no trains by force. They were simply to refuse to handle Pullmans.

The managers' first move was to bring in scabs. With millions made jobless by the depression, it wasn't hard to find strikebreakers.

The next step was to arrange for troops to be called out. The managers knew this would make the public think of the strike not as a labor-capital dispute but as a labor-government battle. They went to the attorney general for help. He was Richard Olney, a railroad lawyer for many years and a board member of several lines. Olney told President Cleveland federal troops were needed to prevent interference with the mails and with interstate commerce. The President said he couldn't sent troops except to enforce a federal court order.

Olney then worked out legal reasons for the courts to intervene. He said the railroads weren't just a private operation but a "public highway." If workers quit as a group on that highway, they were conspiring to obstruct commerce. He picked Edwin Walker, another railroad lawyer, and made him special federal attorney in Chicago to carry out that end of his plan. He wired Walker:

> I FEEL THAT THE TRUE WAY OF DEALING WITH THE
> MATTER IS BY A FORCE WHICH IS OVERWHELMING AND
> PREVENTS ANY ATTEMPT AT RESISTANCE.

He told Walker he didn't have to wait for criminal or illegal acts to get court action. He could ask the court for a ruling to prevent persons from interfering with the mails in violation of the Sherman Anti-Trust Act.

With two federal judges, Walker worked out a sweeping injunction against all strike activity. The injunction was a legal device to bar Debs and all members of the American Railway Union from interfering with the mails, with interstate commerce or with the operations of the 23 railroads now involved in the strike. At the same time Walker increased the marshal's force from 50 to 1,000 men.

The unions were bitter. Federal power was being involved to break the strike. Why wasn't it being used to get George Pullman to negotiate?

When a marshal read the injunction to a crowd gathered along the railroad tracks, he was hooted and his deputies roughhoused. Immediately, Walker wired Washington for troops. By President Cleveland's order, federal troops marched into Chicago on July 4. Governor Altgeld protested the move as unnecessary and unconstitutional. Walker swore in another 2,600 special deputies, selected, armed and paid for by the railroads and called by the Chicago police "thugs, thieves and ex-convicts."

Now the violence the Association hoped for began. Excited crowds flocked to the railway yards and open street fighting took place. With 14,000 men under arms, the city was like a military camp. The militia shot into crowds trying to stop the movement of trains, and a score or more were killed. Flaming freight cars lit up the night skies. By July 6, 1894, the city was near hysteria. MOB IS IN CONTROL, ran the headlines. LAW IS TRAMPLED ON ... STRIKE IS NOW WAR.

Debs said again and again—and local officials backed him up—that the rioting was being done by hooligans, not by strikers. But the press ignored his charges, calling him drunkard and dictator. Across the country editorials began talking darkly of revolution. "The attitude of Debs and his followers is that of rebellion and anarchy," said the *New York Times*. And the New York *Herald* added, Debs "is at war, not with corporations, or with capital, but with the U.S. government and all government."

With the armed power of the government and the court's injunction thrown against them, the strikers became discouraged. The boycott was near defeat. Debs had refused to obey the injunction, knowing it meant giving up the strike. While Pullman refused to arbitrate, the workers had no other way to defend their interests. A grand jury indicted Debs for conspiracy. Out on bail and desperate, he turned to the trade unions for support. Alarmed by the prospect of a general strike, Gompers came to town. Debs told him there was no longer any chance for victory and asked him to get the General Managers' Association to agree to take back the strikers without discrimination. Gompers refused.

As the press shrieked, FRENZIED MOB STILL BENT ON DEATH AND DESTRUCTION, some 700 union leaders were arrested. Debs was thrown into jail for six months for violating the injunction.

The strike was broken.

The American Railway Union was smashed.

What scabs and soldiers could not do for the employers, the injunction had done.

The injunction was nothing new. But the use made of it in the Pullman strike turned it into a devastating weapon against labor. The Supreme Court's ruling on the Debs case meant that an employer didn't have to rely on violence to break a strike. He could simply claim that his sales would be hurt by strikes, picketing or boycotts.

From then on, no sooner was a strike call sounded than it was followed in most cases by a state or federal court injunction. One judge prohibited a craft federation from promoting or endorsing a strike "in any manner by letters, printed or other circulars, telegrams or telephones, word of mouth, oral persuasion, or suggestion, or through interviews to be published in newspapers."

What this did to the First Amendment and a person's right to free speech the judge didn't say.

A striker couldn't even raise his voice in protest. One court said he was in contempt if caught

inducing or attempting to induce by use of threats, violent or abusive language, opprobrious epithets, physical violence or threats thereof, intimidations, display of numbers or force, jeers, entreaties, argument, persuasion, rewards or otherwise any person or persons to abandon the employment of said railway companies or any of them or to refrain from entering such employment . . . engaging, directing, or encouraging others to engage in the practice commonly known as picketing . . . congregating at or near any of the yards, shops, depots, terminals, tracks, roadbeds or premises . . . going singly or collectively to the homes, abodes or places of residence of any employee of said railway . . .

As if that weren't enough, one court in Boston ruled that the United Shoe Workers were forbidden to "side with or in any way encourage or pay strike benefits" to any of its own members who had walked off a job. The workers called this the "starvation injunction."

For some time now American workers had been learning that their government was not impartial in disputes between labor and capital. In the Pullman boycott federal power was placed solidly on the side of the employers.

Did Pullman end labor's hopes of making gains through industrial unionism?

No. For the Debs union showed itself strong enough to match the network of railroads united against it. What defeated it was not the corporations themselves, but their ability to muster the federal army and the court injunction on their side.

15

REFORMERS AND RADICALS

The defeat of the Pullman strike did not end public discussion of what it all meant. A federal commission was appointed by President Cleveland to investigate the causes of the great struggle. It took testimony from railroad officials and labor leaders, from strikers and public servants. After hearing more than a hundred witnesses, the commission said the final responsibility for the Pullman boycott "rests with the people themselves and with the government for not adequately controlling monopoly and corporations, and for failing to reasonably protect the rights of labor and redress its wrongs."

The commission's report was a sign of an important change in the way people thought.

Jane Addams sensed what was happening. She was that remarkable woman who established Hull House settlement in the midst of Chicago's slums only a few years before the Pullman boycott. George Pullman, she said, saw virtue only in the ruthless individualism that had brought him to the top and failed to understand that

the social passion of the age is directed toward the eman-
cipation of the wage-worker; that a great accumulation of
moral force is overmastering men and making for this
emancipation as in another time it made for the emanci-

*pation of the slave; that nothing will satisfy the aroused
conscience of men short of the complete participation of the
working classes in the spiritual, intellectual and material
inheritance of the human race.*

This was a new wind blowing. You could see its direction
in the statement made by a group of young American
economists:

*We regard the state as an educational and ethical agency
whose positive aid is an indispensable condition to human
progress.*

Labor should be treated equally, they said; wages
should be fair, prices just and working conditions decent.

Here and there the church too began to look at the social
world with a fresh eye. By the mid-1880s a new movement
was afoot among the churchmen. Opposed to the "gospel
of wealth," it called itself the "social gospel." Ministers
demanded that the church examine social issues and work
for reforms. If the church wanted to win back the confidence of the masses, it had to stop being an apologist for
wealth and power.

Preaching in Hell's Kitchen amid New York's worst
slums, Walter Rauschenbusch said he had seen how

*man is treated as a thing to produce more things. Men are
hired as hands and not as men. They are paid only enough
to maintain their working capacity and not enough to
develop their manhood. When their working force is exhausted, they are flung aside without consideration of their
human needs. Jesus asked, "Is not a man more than a
sheep?" Our industry says "No."*

By this time many Americans had already been reading
books that opened their eyes to the realities. Among the
first was Henry George's *Progress and Poverty*, published
in 1879. This passionate portrait of hard times sold a
hundred editions and made millions of people concerned
about the inequality in American life. In 1887 came Edward Bellamy's *Looking Backward*, a utopian novel set in

the year 2000. It showed what life could be like if the social, economic and political system were organized to eliminate poverty, disease and corruption. Countless Americans read it and absorbed its lessons.

In 1892 came a new program for making America over. This time it was not the work of one lonely thinker but the voice of a million. As business and labor organized in the generation that followed the Civil War, the farmer slowly followed their example. The natural calamities of drought and pestilence had always made his lot hard. But now the railroads, the mortgage companies, the trusts, and the middlemen were making life unbearable. He was feeding a continent but he had nothing to show for his labor. Discontent turned into organization.

At Omaha, Nebraska on July 4, 1892, some 1,300 delegates joined to launch the new Populist or People's Party. Across the stage was flung their banner: WE DO NOT ASK FOR SYMPATHY OR PITY: WE ASK FOR JUSTICE.

The convention adopted a radical program, with a platform that declared:

Wealth belongs to him who creates it, and every dollar taken from industry without an equivalent is robbery. "If any will not work, neither shall he eat." The interests of rural and civil labor are the same; their enemies are identical.

We believe that the time has come when the railroad corporations will either own the people or the people must own the railroads . . . Transportation being a means of exchange and a public necessity, the government should own and operate the railroads in the interest of the people . . . The telegraph and telephone, like the post office system, being a necessity for the transmission of news, should be owned and operated by the government in the interest of the people.

The new party got nearly a million votes that year, or 8.5% of the ballots cast. The Democrat Grover Cleveland won the presidency, but the Populists elected governors in Colorado, Kansas, North Dakota and Wyoming; sent two senators and 11 congressmen to Washington; and sat 354 representatives in 19 state legislatures.

In the next presidential election the Populists combined with the radical wing of the Democratic Party behind William Jennings Bryan. He lost by a close margin, but in a few years the Populists' call for bold action to curb organized wealth and to equalize opportunity would be debated by major candidates everywhere. They raised a curtain on a period of American life that would be called the Progressive Era. The railroad strike of 1877, the eight-hour fight and the Haymarket hangings, the lockout at Homestead and the Pullman strike had left their mark on national thinking. America began to see wage earners and their struggles in a new light.

A group of journalists played a great role in this awakening. The work of the "muckrakers," as they were early called, appeared in several magazines of mass circulation. These journalists were not exposing isolated conditions. They were talking about what was wrong with the whole of American society. They named names and places. Often they took their information from court records and Congressional investigations.

Thousands of muckraking articles and many books appeared in the years 1902 to 1912. A good part of them were the work of some dozen writers who made this reform journalism their specialty. One of the best known, Upton Sinclair, created a muckraking classic in his novel *The Jungle*. It was based on his investigation of conditions in the Chicago stockyards. Another was Robert Hunter's book *Poverty*, which showed there were at least 10 million people in America who were "underfed, underclothed, and poorly housed."

The muckrakers helped make the country take stock of where it was going. They reawakened conscience and started people thinking once more of what their duties were in the development of a free and democratic society.

By 1900 there were so many thinking this way, they became a movement called the Progressives. They had no single blueprint for a better society. They differed from each other in many ways. But all wanted to see the promise of American life fulfilled for the masses.

There was still a long way to go.

In 1910 nearly eight million women and about two million children were earning wages outside the home. Nearly half the women averaged no more that $6 a week. Some 40% of the children held jobs where conditions were the worst and the employers the most ruthless—in mines, factories, textile mills, tenement workshops. In the clothing industry children's wages averaged $2 a week; in the glass and silk industries it was less than $3 a week. Almost half the boys worked a 10-hour day.

As for the men, three-fourths of all employed in industry earned under $15 a week in 1915. Hours still ranged up to 12 a day, seven days a week, in steel and railroads. The average working day was 10 hours, six days a week. Not many workers were enjoying an eight-hour day. The industrial accident rate was appalling. In 1914, a federal report said, 35,000 workers were killed, "and at least one-half these deaths were preventable." Another 700,000 were injured every year.

With the muckrakers in the lead, the Progressives did all they could to spread information about social evils and to urge citizens to use the ballot to change things. Their numbers and influence became so great that in 1912 the former president, Theodore Roosevelt, took over leadership of the new Progressive Party and ran for the presidency again. He lost, beaten by the Democrat Woodrow Wilson.

One of Wilson's first executive acts was to appoint a federal commission to investigate the ever-mounting violence between capital and labor.

Questioning almost a thousand witnesses, the probers gathered over six million words of testimony. After reporting the facts on how badly workers were paid and how poorly they lived, the commission looked into the distribution of wealth:

Massed in millions at the other end of the social scale are fortunes of a size never before dreamed of, whose very owners do not know the extent nor, without the aid of an intelligent clerk, even the sources of their income . . .

The ownership of wealth in the U.S. has become concentrated to a degree which is difficult to grasp. The "Rich," 2

percent of the people, own 35 percent of the wealth. The
"Poor," 65 percent of the people, own 5 percent of the wealth.
The actual concentration, however, has been carried much
further than these figures indicate. The largest private
fortune in the U.S., estimated at one billion dollars, is
equivalent to the aggregate wealth of 2,500,000 of those
who are classed as "Poor," who are shown to own on the
average about $400 each.

In the face of such inequality, some thought reform was
not enough. They worked for radical change in society.
Eugene Debs, sitting in prison after the Pullman strike,
began to question whether labor could ever gain anything
real and lasting under the capitalist system. Thinking
about his experiences as worker and trade unionist, he
came out of jail converted. "The issue is Socialism versus
Capitalism," he said. "I am for Socialism because I am for
humanity."

For three decades socialist groups had struggled to find
a following in America. In 1901 Debs joined with others in
forming the Socialist Party of America. In 1904 he drew
400,000 votes for president. By 1912 the party itself had
enrolled 118,000 members, and Debs rolled up nearly a
million votes for president. The Socialists had 13 daily
newspapers, 42 weeklies and their own school and publishing house. They won many successes in elections. At
one time over a thousand of their members held public
office, capturing the mayoralty of such large cities as
Milwaukee and electing congressmen, state and city legislators.

Their long-range goal was the cooperative common-
wealth, but their success came because they worked hard for
immediate demands, for reforms that could be realized now.

At first the Socialists tried to win labor's support
through the American Federation of Labor. (It had over
half a million members in 1900.) At its 1902 convention a
Socialist motion to commit the Federation to collective
ownership of the means of production lost by a close
margin of five to four. But though the Socialists made
many converts within the unions, Gompers was dead set
against them.

Many of the radical unionists gave up all hope of push-
ing the American Federation of Labor into a more militant
struggle against the corporations. That was how the Industrial Workers of the World was born. Its aim was to put
the working class in control of economic power. The Industrial Workers of the World's platform was direct:

*The working class and the employing class have nothing
in common. There can be no peace so long as hunger and
want are found among millions of working people and the
few, who make up the employing class, have all the good
things of life . . .*
*It is the historic mission of the working class to do away
with capitalism. The army of production must be organized, not only for the every-day struggle with capitalists,
but also to carry on production when capitalism shall have
2been overthrown. By organizing industrially we are forming the structure of the new society within the shell of the
old.*

In the founding convention of the Industrial Workers of
the World at Chicago in 1905, several prominent Socialists
took part, as well as such labor leaders as Big Bill Haywood, president of the Western Federation of Miners, and
Mother Jones, the labor organizer. The Industrial Workers of the World opposed the craft unionism and the
caution of the American Federation of Labor. It went out
to organize all workers, regardless of trade, skill, race or
sex, into industrial unions.

Most of the Industrial Workers of the World's organizing was done in the West, among the migratory workers,
the lumber workers and the farm laborers. In the East the
Industrial Workers of the World gave leadership to immigrant workers neglected by the American Federation of
Labor. The biggest test of the Industrial Workers of the
World came in 1912 in a Massachusetts textile center.

16

BREAD— AND ROSES TOO!

The place is Lawrence, Massachusetts, the biggest textile town in the world.

The time is Friday, January 12, 1912.

Suddenly, labor editor Justus Ebert reports, something extraordinary is happening in the mills:

About 9 A.M. on that date, the employees in one of the departments of the Everett Mill swept through its long floors, wildly excited, carrying an American flag which they waved amid shouts of "Strike! Strike!! All out! Come on, all out! Strike! Strike!!" From room to room they rushed, an enraged, indignant mass. Arming themselves with the picker sticks used in the mills, they went from loom to loom, persuading and driving away operatives, stopping looms, tearing weaves, and smashing machines where repeated attempts were made to run them despite their entreaties, which seldom failed of instant response. As they swept on, their numbers grew, and with them grew the contagion, the uproar and the tumult.

Out of the Everett Mill they rushed, these hundreds of peaceful workers, now aroused, passionate and tense. On the street, outside of the mill gates, they were met by excited crowds that were congregated there. All of them coalesced into one big mass, and as such, moved over the Union Street bridge on to Wood, Washington and Ayer Mills, where the same scenes were enacted once more. Men, women and children—Italians, Poles, Syrians—all races, all creeds, already aroused to action before the coming of the crowd outside (some of whom rushed the gates and entered), ran through the thousands of feet of floor space, shouting "Strike! Strike!! Strike!!! All out! Strike! Strike!! Strike!!!" sweeping everything before them, and rendering operation in many departments so impossible as to cause their complete shutdown.

These thousands also poured out into the streets, and with their fellow workers already assembled there, choked up the highway, blocking cars and suspending traffic generally, while at the same time hooting and howling, raising speakers and leaders on their shoulders, throwing ice and snow, and bombarding the windows in the adjoining Kuhnhardt and Duck Mills, smashing every pane of glass there—a destructive, menacing mob. Where peace had reigned before, disorder and violence now seemed rampant.

It was an industrial revolt. The mill workers had risen. The great Lawrence strike was under way.

To Lawrence came one of the most brilliant muckrakers. He was Ray Stannard Baker, a University of Michigan graduate. He had recently added to his fame as a great reporter by investigating the living and working conditions of blacks in American life; his findings were put in a book, *Following the Color Line.*

What started the revolt in Lawrence? Baker reported what he found in the *American Magazine*:

Upon that day, in the Washington mill of the so-called Woolen Trust, a handful of Italian operatives had gone to draw their pay envelopes. Of all the mingled peoples of Lawrence, none are so humble as the Italians, none so eager for work at any price, and none so ill-paid. They are the last and the poorest of the successive waves of people from Europe which have been surging upon our shores during the last thirty years. When these people opened their envelopes, they found that there was a reduction of pay corre-

sponding to two hours of work in a week—the price, per-
haps, of three or four loaves of bread. A small matter,
indeed, the comfortably fed outsider may observe, but in
Lawrence, where many adult workers make only $6 to
$7.50 a week, it is not an unimportant matter. A matter,
indeed, of very great importance!

"It was like a spark of electricity," an overseer described
it to me.

It changed instantly the discipline of years: it brought
about sudden wild confusion. One of the bosses, attempting
to restore order with the threat formerly as potent as magic,
shouted to one of the Italians:

"Tony, if you don't get back to your place, you'll lose your
job."

"To hell with the job," responded Tony. "I'll pitch it."

And "pitch it" they did. They swept out of the mill, taking
hundreds of others with them, they marched to other mills
and called out hundreds more. On the way a few belts were
cut, a few windows broken—losses not serious in them-
selves, but symbolic of the temper of the men, suggestive of
future possibilities. And with marching and singing
through the main streets of the town the strike began.

The immediate cause of the strike was a wage cut. A
state law had just been passed reducing the hours of
women and children from 56 to 54 a week. The employers
had strongly opposed it because over half of the 40,000
workers in the woolen and cotton mills were in these
categories. Now they cut wages proportionately, and at the
same time speeded up the machines so that for 54 hours
at 54 hours' pay they got the same output they used to get
in 56 hours at 56 hours' pay.

The difference in pay was only the price of a good
Havana cigar for the mill owners. But workers were already at the starvation point. "Better to starve fighting
than to starve working," was now their battle cry, shouted
in a score of tongues. For one of the unique aspects of the
Lawrence strike was the great variety of people involved
in it. There were at least 30 different nationalities in the
city, speaking some 45 different languages. The largest
groups were Italians, Germans and French Canadians.

Then there were Poles, Lithuanians, Franco-Belgians, Syrians and a sprinkling of Russians, Jews, Greeks, Letts and Turks. About half Lawrence was foreign born, but only about 8% of the mill workers were native born.

The mill owners invited foreign labor in, but they kept out foreign business competition. For 50 years they had enjoyed the benefits of a tariff law that kept foreign-made goods from coming into the country. The effect? Ray Stannard Baker found out:

For the workmen it meant the lowest possible standards of living. Men with large families had to compete with adventurous single men and unmarried girls. No man can support a family on $300 or $400 a year even though he lives in the meanest way. The result was that the wife also had to go into the mills, followed by one child after another, as fast as they arrived at the legal age. It took the combined earnings of many members of the family to feed and clothe the family. This meant the break-up of all decent family life and all effort toward real civilized development. It meant living in dark tenements; it meant taking in lodgers to the point of indecent crowding. Some of the tenements of Lawrence are the worst I ever saw. Statistics show that the rentals in Lawrence are almost as high (95 percent) as those in the enormously larger city of New York; and that food prices are higher (105 percent) than those in New York—these figures being from the report of the British Board of Trade.

I did not find any cases of actual and immediate starvation such as were reported in certain newspapers, but it is an undoubted fact that there is an appalling amount of underfeeding. I asked the ages of many young people I met and they looked (and they were) stunted, not fully developed. Thousands, also in this city which often suffers from overproduction of cloth, go underclad: in the crowds of strikers in the streets on those bitter March mornings, the number I saw without overcoats and evidently too thinly clad, was very great. And in their homes, wherever I went, the tendency was to crowd into the kitchen and save coal by keeping only one room warm.

The result of all this is a high death-rate, especially from
diseases resulting from exposure and poor sanitary condi-
tions—like pneumonia. Also, the young children die at an
appalling rate (169 per 1,000).

The system was bad for the workers. But how did it
affect the mill owners? The Pacific Mills was paying 12%
dividends regularly. The American Woolen Company—
the largest single corporation in textiles, with 34 mills—
was paying 7% and the Arlington, 8%. All this, and extra
dividends and surpluses, too.

Seeking domination of the textile industry, each mill in
recent years had been speeding up both workers and
machinery. First, weavers were forced to attend two looms
instead of one. Then the speed of the machinery was
gradually but steadily increased. For the workers it became an exhausting, killing struggle. Wages slowly advanced over the years, but not as fast as the cost of living.

And most importantly for men out to make the highest
profits, the product per worker in cloth increased much
faster than wages. That difference went to the stockholders, not to labor.

Who were these stockholders? Mr. Baker studied them:

Among them are some of the finest people in New En-
gland. Many live in Boston, and are among the most
cultured and delightful people in the world. Among them
are representatives of some of the strong old families of
Massachusetts, such names as Lowell, Lawrence, Lyman,
Coolidge, Amory, Ayer. It can almost be said that the
aristocracy of Boston is based upon the profits of the textile
mills of New England. Now, like so many rich people in
this country, they seem to be far more sensitive to the
responsibilities of the possession of great wealth than to the
ethics of making it. Many of them are interested in "all good
works." I know as a fact that there are no people in the
country who have contributed more liberally to the educa-
tion and uplift of Southern Negroes, to missions in Hawaii,
and to many other good causes than these men of Boston.
But about conditions in the dark alleys of Lawrence, where
their own money comes from—apparently they know very

little, nor do they want to know. Here, indeed, is an aston-
ishing fact, which I feel like having printed in large letters:

NOT A SINGLE LARGE STOCKHOLDER IN
THE LAWRENCE MILLS LIVES IN LAWRENCE.
NOT ONE.

A textile working town is not a pleasant place to live
in—dirty wooden buildings, dirty streets, unlovely looking
people, cheap goods in the store windows, no good society.
So the owners live in Boston and elsewhere . . . Drive out
from Lawrence in almost any direction and you will see the
fine homes of these people crowning all the hills. They will
tell you what a fine government they have under the dem-
ocratic town meeting systems in Methuen and Andover as
compared with the corrupt government of Lawrence. And
you will find the very people who have deserted Lawrence,
where all their property interests are located, excoriating
the corrupt political conditions of the city . . .
Thus the workers of Lawrence have been in large mea-
sure deserted, neglected and forgotten by the very men who
profit most by their labor. There is no spirit of cooperation
between the men who own the mills and the men who work
in them.

With all their grievances, the workers of Lawrence had
never been organized. The American Federation of Labor
had enrolled about 200 of the skilled workers in its craft
locals. But these were only a handful, and all were the
English- speaking aristocracy of the textile trades. The
many thousands of unskilled workers were never touched.

One union, however—the new Industrial Workers of the
World—had been trying to organize Lawrence since as far
back as 1905. But not until 1911 did it begin to make
headway. Baker describes how:

The basic idea upon which the Industrial Workers of the
World is organized is a very big one. They seek to bring
together not merely the workers in any one craft, but all the
workers in all industries. It is not the Brotherhood of
Engineers, or the Brotherhood of Printers, or of Wool-Sort-

*ers that they preach, but the Brotherhood of all workers.
They advocate not the horizontal stratification of labor
along lines of craft and skill, but the perpendicular stratification along lines of industry. They say that the veriest
bobbin boy is as essential a cog in the machinery of production as the highest skilled wool-sorter. They say that the
old craft organizations tend to become exclusive and mo-
nopolistic: that they keep out apprentices, limit output,
make agreements with employers which benefit only themselves, and even combine with employers to mulct the
public. They say that all workers should unite just as all
capital is uniting, and that so long as the workers do not
stand together they will be defeated. Right or wrong, this
is their platform.*

One of the Industrial Workers of the World organizers
who came to Lawrence—21-year-old Elizabeth Gurley
Flynn—wrote about the way William D. Haywood, the
organization's leader, pointed up this difference when he
spoke to workers:

*They roared with laughter and applause when he said:
"The A.F. of L. organizes like this!"—separating his fingers, as far apart as they would go, and naming them—
"weavers, loom-fixers, dyers, spinners." Then he would say:
"The I.W.W. organizes like this!"—tightly clenching his big
fist, shaking it at the bosses.*

The Industrial Workers of the World had its own way of
organizing workers and conducting a strike. It brought in
several of its best people—26-year-old Joseph Ettor, who
could talk with workers in Italian, English or Polish, even
Hungarian and Yiddish, and Arturo Giovannitti, 27, a
former coal miner and teacher, now a labor editor, poet
and orator.

The Industrial Workers of the World held mass meetings in every part of town, talking to the different language
groups with the help of translators. All the groups elected
delegates to the strike committee that represented every
mill and every department, as well as every nationality.
The strikers met on the Lawrence Common, or public

square, so that the workers could feel their size and power and unity. Soon Haywood—a huge, rocklike man, with a big head and a booming voice—arrived to help, and was met at the station by 15,000 workers.

The city was now an armed camp. For the first time in the history of Massachusetts labor disputes, the state sent in 1,400 militiamen to back up the police and state troopers. Clashes took place almost daily between them and the strikers. Thousands of strikers formed an endless chain picket line that circled the mills. They wore white arm bands reading Don't Be a Scab.

On January 30 in a battle between pickets and police a woman striker was killed. Although Ettor and Giovannitti were miles away, they were arrested and jailed, together with Joseph Caruso, one of the pickets. The three were charged with being accessories to murder because their speeches had advocated picketing.

It was the same theory of conspiracy used to convict the Haymarket speakers.

Other Industrial Workers of the World leaders took charge of the strike, with Haywood elected chairman of the strike committee.

The Industrial Workers of the World was much abused by the mill owners and the press. The organizers were called "agitators," "Socialists," "anarchists." They were "outsiders" blamed for coming in to disturb contented workers. How contented the workers were the scale and passion of the revolt showed. But it was true that the Industrial Workers of the World had goals different from those of the familiar union strike. That kind of strike demanded higher wages or better working conditions. Baker reported:

> The strike at Lawrence . . . was far more than a revolt; it was an incipient revolution. It was revolutionary because it involved a demand for fundamental changes in the basic organization of industry. Thinly veiled behind its demands for higher wages lay the outspoken declaration of the leaders for abolition of the entire wage system, and the suppression of the private ownership of capital. In so many words the organization declares its position:

"Instead of the conservative motto, 'A fair day's wage for a fair day's work,' we must inscribe on our banner the revolutionary watchword, 'Abolition of the wage system!'"

In short, this was a Socialist strike as contrasted with the familiar craft or trade-union strike of the past.

There was something else new and different about this strike. The reporters who descended upon Lawrence from many places discovered a vital, intense spirit in the workers—"a religious spirit, if you will," as one put it—that was amazing. Baker observed that

this movement in Lawrence was strongly a singing movement. It is the first strike I ever saw which sang. I shall not soon forget the curious lift, the strange sudden fire of the mingled nationalities at the strike meetings when they broke into the universal language of song. And not only at the meetings did they sing, but at the soup houses and in the streets. I saw one group of women strikers, who were peeling potatoes at a relief station suddenly break into the swing of "The Internationale." They have a whole book of songs fitted to familiar tunes—the "Eight-hour Song," "Banner of Labor," "Workers, Shall the Masters Rule Us?" and so on—but the favorite of all was the Socialist song called "The Internationale":

> *Arise, ye prisoners of starvation!*
> *   Arise, ye wretched of the earth,*
> *For justice thunders condemnation,*
> *   A better world's in birth.*
> *No more tradition's chains shall bind us,*
> *   Rise, ye slaves! no more in thrall!*
> *The earth shall rise on new foundations,*
> *   We have been naught, we shall be all.*

> REFRAIN

> *'Tis the final conflict,*
> *   Let each stand in his place,*
> *The Industrial Union*
> *   Shall be the human race.*

Besides the daily meeting of strikers, Haywood held special meetings of women and children. He used simple, down-to-earth language and made sure the foreign-born workers understood him. He helped the women overcome their husbands' idea that women should stay at home and not go on the picket line or to meetings. You are strikers as well as wives and mothers, he said, and you are just as brave fighters as your men. They proved him right.

As the bitter New England winter wore on, the violence against the strikers got worse. In mid-February, 200 police clubbed a picket line of 100 women. Women with nursing babies were sent to jail.

The strikers had no savings and the Industrial Workers of the World had no treasury. Fuel and food were needed badly. Traveling strike committees found friends among the workers of many other mill towns, and funds and food came in fast. Then the strikers adopted a method used successfully in Europe—sending the workers' children away to be cared for by strike supporters in other cities. Mrs. Flynn tells what happened:

The parents accepted the idea and the children were wild to go. On February 17, the first group of 150 children were taken to New York City. A small group also left for Barre, Vermont. A New York Committee came to Lawrence to escort them. Five thousand people met them at Grand Central Station. People wept when they saw the poor clothes and thin shoes of these wide-eyed little children. They picked them up and carried them on their shoulders to the El Station. They were taken to the Labor Temple of East 84th Street, where they were fed, and examined by 15 volunteer doctors, then turned over to their eager hosts, all of whom had been carefully checked by the committee. There were not enough children, and many New Yorkers left disappointed not to be able to have a Lawrence child. There was a long waiting list, until another group came later . . . The letters the children wrote home glowed with accounts of their new warm clothes and how well they were treated. The Lawrence children were sent to school in New York, including those who had worked in the mills . . . When they finally returned to Lawrence at the end of the strike, they were loaded down with clothing, toys, presents and clothes for their families from their New York friends.

The children's exodus was a dramatic move and caught the attention of the nation as nothing else had. The Lawrence authorities did not like all the publicity and feared it would help prolong the strike. Their anger led to their worst mistake, described by Mrs. Flynn:

On February 24, a group of 40 strikers' children were to go from Lawrence to Philadelphia. A committee came from there to escort them, including a young Sunday school teacher. At the railroad station in Lawrence, where the children were assembled, accompanied by their fathers and mothers, just as they were ready to board the train, they were surrounded by police. Troopers surrounded the station outside to keep others out. Children were clubbed and torn away from their parents and a wild scene of brutal disorder took place. Thirty-five frantic women and children were arrested, thrown screaming and fighting into patrol wagons. They were beaten into submission and taken to the police station. There the women were charged with "neglect" and improper guardianship and ten frightened children taken to the Lawrence Poor Farm. The police station was besieged by enraged strikers. Members of the Philadelphia Committee were arrested and fined.

The whole country was shocked by the news from Lawrence. Judge Ben Lindsey of Colorado said it "shows the depravity and greed and the inhumanity of our industrial system." Senator Borah called the police action "an invasion of constitutional privileges." Novelist William Dean Howells said, "It is an outrage—could anyone think it was anything else?"

The attack on women and children led to a Congressional investigation of the strike in March. More than 50 strikers—many of them children—went to Washington to tell their stories and display their pay envelopes. Mrs. William Howard Taft, the president's wife, was at the hearing. She listened to a pregnant striker tell how she

was beaten by Lawrence police and to a Lawrence minister
testify that "fourteen is not too young for children to work
in the mill." The country's indignation mounted. Later,
President Taft approved an investigation of labor conditions throughout the nation.

The mill owners were worried by public reaction. They
feared it might lead to removal of the tariff protecting their
industry and ensuring its profits. On March 12, 1912, the
American Woolen Company gave in to all the strikers'
demands. By the end of the month the rest of the mills fell
in line. Wages throughout the New England textile industry were raised 5 to 20%. In Lawrence there was to be more
pay for overtime, too, and no discrimination against any
striker. Twenty thousand workers assembled on the common to celebrate the victory.

Meanwhile, Ettor, Giovannitti and Caruso still sat in
jail. Months dragged by without a trial. Protest parades
and demonstrations throughout the country raised
$60,000 for their legal defense. In September a 24-hour
strike by 15,000 Lawrence workers finally led to the men's
trial. It lasted for two months, with the defendants—pre-
sumed to be innocent until proved guilty—kept in metal
cages in the courtroom. On November 26 they were acquit-
ted by the jury and freed.

What was the result of the 10-week strike in Lawrence?
Baker said:

> It was called a great victory for the strikers. But has
> anything really been settled? The head of the family who was
> getting $6 or $7 a week before the strike, and as a result of
> victory received ten percent increase in wages, is still below
> the breadline, is still far below civilized standards. He and
> his family can live 60 or 70 cents a week better—but consider
> if you will, how very little 60 or 70 cents a week really means
> in bread, in rent, in clothing, in fuel, for a family of children.
> After all, is not the conclusion forced upon us that the changes
> have got to be different and deeper?

Another observer saw something else in that strike.
Literary critic Kenneth McGowan, writing in Forum Magazine, said:

THE GENERAL STRIKE IS THE KEY THAT FITS THE LOCK TO FREEDOM

When the Lawrence strike leaders Ettor and Giovanitti were jailed, their union paper published this cartoon calling for a general strike to free them. (Courtesy New York Public Library)

Whatever its future, the IWW has accomplished one tremendously big thing, a thing that sweeps away all twaddle over red flags and violence and sabotage, and that is the individual awakening of "illiterates" and "scum" to an original, personal conception of society and the realization of the dignity and rights of their part in it. They have learned more than class consciousness; they have learned consciousness of self.

Perhaps one of the best expressions of the great Lawrence strike is the poem "Bread and Roses." It was written by James Oppenheim when he saw young mill girls picketing with a banner that read, "We want bread and roses too."

Bread and Roses

*As we come marching, marching in the beauty
   of the day,
A million darkened kitchens, a thousand mill
   lofts gray,
Are touched with all the radiance that a sudden
   sun discloses,
For the people hear us singing: "Bread and
   roses! Bread and roses!"*

*As we come marching, marching, we battle too
   for men,
For they are women's children, and we mother
   them again.
Our lives shall not be sweated from birth until
   life closes;
Hearts starve as well as bodies; give us bread,
   but give us roses!*

*As we come marching, marching, unnumbered
   women dead
Go crying through our singing their ancient cry
   for bread.
Small art and love and beauty their drudging
   spirits knew.
Yes, it is bread we fight for—but we fight for
   roses, too!*

*As we come marching, marching, we bring the
    greater days.*
*The rising of the women means the rising of
    the race.*
*No more the drudge and idler—ten that toil
    where one reposes,*
*But a sharing of life's glories: Bread and roses!
    Bread and roses!*

17

MASSACRE AT LUDLOW

Arturo Giovannitti, the labor organizer, is addressing the jury at the close of his trial in 1912 for inciting the workers to violence during the strike at Lawrence:

If there was any violence in Lawrence . . . it was not my fault. If you must go back to the origin of all the trouble, gentlemen of the jury, you will find that the origin and reason was the wage system. It was the infamous rule of domination of one man by another man . . . It is the same principle . . . that made a man at that time a chattel slave, a soulless human being, a thing that could be bought and bartered and sold, and which now, having changed the term, makes the same man—but a white man—the slave of the machine.

They say that you are free in this great and wonderful country . . . But I say you cannot be half free and half slave, and economically all the working class in the United States are as much slaves now as the Negroes were forty and fifty years ago; because the man that owns the tools wherewith another man works, the man that owns the house where this man lives, the man that owns the factory where this man wants to go to work—that man owns and controls the bread that that man eats and therefore owns and controls his mind, his body, his heart and his soul.

What was Giovannitti talking about? Was this true of American workers? Now, in the twentieth century?

The man that owns the tools, the house, the factory, the bread
of another man owns that man's mind, body, heart, soul . . .

Within a year the whole country would see a living
demonstration of those words. It took place more than
2,000 miles away from Lawrence, Massachusetts in coal
fields on the eastern slope of the Rocky Mountains. Here,
in southern Colorado, in September 1913, a 15-month
strike began that was much more than a union battle for
better wages. It was a revolt against industrial slavery.
The causes of the strike lay deep, reported John A. Fitch
in the *Survey*, and "Congress and the whole country should
know them":

First, there is the feudal system of community control,
as in Alabama, West Virginia, and in certain districts in
Pennsylvania. The land belongs to the company. The
houses on the land belong to the company. The streets in
the mining camps, the road furnishing often the only
means of egress—all are owned by the company. It is rare
that a miner can buy a house or a foot of ground if he wishes
to do so.

He is therefore absolutely under company control. The
streets are patrolled by armed guards who protect company
property and exercise all the authority there is in the camp.
The miner knows no other government . . . The guards have
a free hand . . . They have acted as policemen and spies, as
union suppressors and as agents for the company stores.
At many camps a stranger is met at the entrance and
compelled by the guard to state his business before being
allowed to enter. And yet these camps are American towns!
Many of the inhabitants are American citizens; but they
cannot receive in their homes, whether as guests or for
business purposes any except those approved tacitly or
otherwise by a man of less than ordinary intelligence and
more than ordinary brutality.

By far the largest coal-mining operator in the region
was the Colorado Fuel and Iron Company. John D. Rockefeller Jr. owned 40% of its stock and bonds and controlled
the company's policies.

After questioning Rockefeller on the causes of the strike, the U.S. Commission on Industrial Relations said:

Such details as wages, working conditions, and the political, social, and moral welfare of the 15,000 or 20,000 inhabitants of his coal camps apparently held no interest for Mr. Rockefeller, for as late as April, 1914, he professed ignorance of these details.

What were those conditions like?

John Reed, a rich young Oregonian recently out of Harvard, was one of the reporters who went to Colorado to see for himself. Reed had just won national fame reporting the Mexican Revolution for *Metropolitan Magazine*. This experience, and his investigations of strike struggles, was turning him toward radical solutions for labor's problems. Later, his eyewitness account of the beginning of the Russian Revolution, *Ten Days That Shook the World*, would become a classic of journalism.

From Colorado, Reed reported first on wages:

The operators give glowing accounts of miners making $5 a day. But the average number of working days a year in Colorado was 191, and the average gross wage of a coal digger was $2.12 a day. In many places it was much lower.

Then, working conditions, rent, cost of living. Again Reed:

Many of these towns were incorporated towns. The mayor of the town was the mine superintendent. The school board was composed of company officials. The only store in town was the company store. All the houses were company houses, rented by the company to the miners. There was no tax on property, and all the property belonged to the mining company. The town was supported by a tax on saloons. Besides that, the miners had to pay a poll-tax of $2 a year. Rent of the unsanitary dilapidated company houses was $2.50 to $3 a month per room.

A miner had to buy his own tools for cash . . . He paid preacher's, school and blacksmithing fees in advance . . .

These must be worked off before he was given any money. If he needed food or clothing or furniture before there was any money to his credit, he went to the company store . . .The price for everything was 25 percent higher than outside the camp.

A principal cause of the strike was the miners' claim that they were being cheated of 500 to 800 pounds of coal on every car they loaded. This excerpt from a state mine inspector's report supports the claim:

March 22, 1912, Colorado Fuel and Iron Company's mine at Morely. Has no check weighman. Find the miners complaining of weights. On inspecting two pairs of scales I find that neither will balance, and that the scales on the south tipple, with 350 pounds, increased the weight of a car of coal only 50 pounds. This is very unsatisfactory to the miners, who claimed that if they asked for a check weighman they would be discharged.

At the C. F. & I. mines at Berwind and Tobasco, I was positively refused to be allowed to examine the scales, and was told that I had nothing to do with them. I found the mine policed by a gunman, who was ready to run anyone out of town that did not suit him.

Accidents are always a major concern to industrial workers, especially to miners. What was the picture in Colorado? A contemporary article in *Harper's Weekly* summed it up:

323 were killed in the Colorado mines in 1910. 163 were left widows, and 303 children were made fatherless. The Congressional Committee developed the fact that no damage suits were ever filed in the coal mine counties, and that it was the habit of permanent coroners' juries to bring in a stereotyped verdict, "Cause of death unknown."

The committee likewise established the fact that two men are killed in the Colorado mines to one in the mines of other states, and that half the accidents were due to the refusal of the coal companies to institute reforms pointed out by inspectors months prior to the disasters.

When asked whether the Rockefeller company had ever thought of setting up a relief fund for injured employees, the company president, J. F. Welborn, replied simply: "No, we never considered the establishment of that."

Congressman Keating of Colorado, calling for a federal investigation, said:

Industrial and political conditions in Las Animas and Huerfano counties have for many years been a menace and a disgrace to our state. For more than ten years the coal companies have owned every official in both counties . . . Business men who have dared to protest have been persecuted and in many cases driven out. The administration of the law has been a farce.

Who were the people who lived under such conditions and struck in the hope of changing them? John Reed described them:

A large part of those who are striking today were brought in as strikebreakers in the great walkout of 1903. Now in that year more than 70 percent of the miners in southern Colorado were English speaking: Americans, English, Scotch and Welsh. Their demands were practically the same as the present ones. Before that, every ten years, back to 1884, there had been similar strikes. Militia and imported mine guards wantonly murdered, imprisoned, and deported out of the state hundreds of miners . . . After the [1903] strike was broken, 10,000 men found themselves blacklisted, for the operators made a careful study of the races most patient under oppression and deliberately imported ignorant foreigners to fill the mines, carefully massing in each mine men of many different languages, who would not be able to organize.

On the eve of the strike there were over 14,000 foreign-born miners in the coal fields, representing 24 nations. The major groups who did not speak English were Italians, Slavs, Austrians, Mexicans, Greeks and Germans. There were also Turks, Montenegrins, Poles, Albanians, Swedes, Russians, Finns, Hungarians, French . . .

The U.S. Labor Bureau charged the corporations with hiring these men "because they can be handled and abused with impunity." That was plainly the opinion of Rockefeller, who said, "Many of these foreigners coming to this country would have very little knowledge of what was the best thing for them."

A union was certainly not good for them. But the miners thought differently. The United Mine Workers—an industrial union not related to the Industrial Workers of the World—had been forced out of Colorado by the defeat of the 1903 strike. In 1911 their organizers came back to open up an office again. Now the union had a national membership of 400,000. It was established in every coal-producing state; 75% of all coal miners in the country worked under contracts that the union had with the operators.

Before calling a strike the United Mine Workers sent the Colorado operators a letter, asking only for a conference: "We are no more desirous of a strike than you are," the letter said, "and it seems to us that we owe it to our respective interests, as well as the general public, to make every honest endeavor to adjust our differences in an enlightened manner."

The mine operators did not reply.

At their state convention, the miners formulated their demands and voted to strike on September 23, unless the operators agreed to open negotiations. The operators ignored all efforts to start talks.

The miners' demands boiled down really to two: that the operators obey the state's mining laws and that they sign a union contract.

On the first point, Welborn, the company president, according to *Harper's Weekly*, admitted before a Congressional committee that

the Colorado law against payment of script, passed in 1897, had not been observed until 1913; that the semimonthly payday ordered by law in 1901, had not been put into effect until 1913; that the eight hour day, adopted in 1905, was a dead letter until 1913; that the law forbidding the deputization of any others save citizens was violated in hundreds of instances when imported desperadoes were

*made deputy sheriffs; and that the law granting miners the
right to have check weighmen was never observed.*

The only reason the operators had just begun to observe
some of these laws was that the union was active again,
and the companies feared a strike.

The mine owners refused to the last moment to deal
with the union. Testimony before the Congressional committee discloses why:

MR. ROCKEFELLER: *It is costing us about $1,000,000 to
stand for the principle which we believe is to the ultimate
interest of those men.*

THE CHAIRMAN: *And that is to fight the union?*

MR. ROCKEFELLER: *That is to allow them to have the
privilege of determining the conditions under which they
shall work . . . When it comes to submitting the question of
whether or not the camps shall be unionized to arbitration,
that is a matter of such basic importance, it is a matter of
such fundamental principle, that we would not feel justified in yielding our view about such a question . . . The
owners of this property . . . would rather see the properties
closed up permanently and lose every dollar of investment
than to concede a point which they believe is so fundamen-
tally against the interest of the workers of the country. It is
a principle we are standing for at any cost.*

On September 23, 1913, the day the strike began, there
was a blizzard. In the bitter cold the mine guards went
through the settlements and threw out all the people who
refused to work. For 50 miles around, out of the mouths of
the canyons straggled the 9,000 striking miners with their
women and children. They trudged through the snow and
sleet to the dozen tent colonies the union had prepared.
The biggest was at Ludlow, along the roads by which
strikebreakers might be brought in.

Earlier the coal companies had imported armed men
from West Virginia, Texas and New Mexico. They were
promptly made deputies by the sheriffs. The U.S. Commission on Industrial Relations investigated the deputies and
reported

that many guards deputized in this illegal fashion and paid by the Colorado Fuel & Iron Company were men of the lowest and most vicious character has been clearly established. That their function was to intimidate and harass the strikers had been demonstrated in the strike of 1903, 1904, and had been made apparent early in the present strike by the shooting to death of Gerald Lippiatt, a union organizer, in the streets of Trinidad immediately after the calling of the strike, by a Baldwin-Felts detective employed by the Colorado Fuel & Iron Company and its associates and deputized by the sheriff of Las Animas County.

How the Baldwin-Felts Detective Agency carried out its assignment at the Forbes tent colony is reported by Henry A. Atkinson, a Congregational Church leader, who went to the strike scene for *Harper's Weekly:*

An armored automobile, made in the shops of the Colorado Fuel & Iron Company, at the suggestion and under the direction of A. C. Felts, manager of the Baldwin-Felts Detective Agency, was brought to Trinidad. This automobile was armed with a Hotchkiss machine gun capable of shooting 400 times a minute, and with a ball that would kill a man at a range of more than a mile. Manned with five deputies, three of them at least being Baldwin-Felts gunmen, this automobile made the trip to the Forbes colony. It stopped just a short distance from the Camp and one of these men took a white handkerchief, put it on the end of a stick and, using it as a flag of truce, approached the group of strikers. As he came up he asked if they were Union men, and receiving their reply in the affirmative, he threw down the flag, jumped to one side and said "Look out for yourselves." At that the machine gun cut loose on the crowd. One hundred and forty-seven bullets were put through one tent; a boy 15 years old was shot nine times in the legs; one miner was killed, shot through the forehead. This was but one of a series of incidents.

The miners, determined to protect themselves against the army of hired gunmen, bought up what few weapons the operators had not already taken. A war between two armed sides had begun. As the U.S. Commission said:

> *In all discussion and thought regarding violence in connection with strike, the seeker after truth must remember that government existed in southern Colorado only as an instrument of tyranny and oppression in the hands of the operators; that, once having dared to oppose that tyranny in a strike, the miners' only protection for themselves and their families lay in the physical force which they could muster.*

In the Ludlow tent colony, reported John Reed:

> *There were more than 1,200 people, divided into 21 nationalities, undergoing the marvelous experience of learning that all men are alike. When they had been living together for two weeks, the petty race prejudices and misunderstandings that had been fostered between them by the coal companies for so many years began to break down. Americans began to find out that Slavs and Italians and Poles were as kind-hearted, as cheerful, as loving and brave as they were. The women called upon one another, boasting about their babies and their men, bringing one another little delicacies when they were sick. The men played cards and baseball together.*
> *"I never did have much use for foreigners before I went to Ludlow," said a little woman. "But they're just like us, only they can't speak the language."*
> *"Sure," answered another. "I used to think Greeks were just common, ignorant, dirty people. But in Ludlow the Greeks were certainly perfect gentlemen. You can't ever say anything bad to me about a Greek now."*
> *Everybody began to learn everybody else's language. And at night there would be a dance in the Big Tent, the Italians supplying the music, and all nations dancing together. It was a true welding of races. These exhausted, beaten, hardworking people had never before had time to know one another ... Twelve hundred souls began to grow.*

Around the tents Reed heard the strikers' children sing this song:

There's a fight in Colorado for to set the miners free,
From the tyrants and the money-kings and all the
    powers that be;
They have trampled on the freedom that was meant
    for you and me,
But Right is marching on.
Cheer boys, cheer the cause of Union,
The Colorado Miners' Union,
Glory, glory to our Union;
Our cause is marching on.

But peace didn't last long. The gunmen threatened they would come down on the colonies and wipe them out. Miners with their few rifles and shotguns stood guard every night over their women and children while company searchlights played ceaselessly on the tents. The guards rode into the colonies, broke up strikers' meetings, shot down miners. The miners fought back. Governor Ammons sent in the National Guard. The guardsmen attacked picket lines, arrested strikers, deported union leaders.

For six months the reign of terror continued. The union made desperate attempts to arrange a conference, but the operators ignored their appeals. Under heavy pressure from the owners, the governor modified his order against importing strikebreakers. Trains came into the state bearing thousands of workers from the East. They had been assured there was no strike, promised free transportation and high wages. The militia, under orders from the mine superintendents, would not let them leave the strike area without permission. Hundreds of strikebreakers escaped at night and fled over the hills in the snow.

As the spring of 1914 came on, three companies of militia were left on duty. They were made up mostly of mine guards, Baldwin-Felts detectives or professional strikebreakers paid by the coal companies.

On Sunday, April 19, the Greek Easter dawned. At Ludlow tent colony everybody celebrated it with the Greeks, starting with dances in national costume, and then baseball games. The Greeks prepared lunch for all the colony. Everybody was happy for a moment, even under the noses of the two machine guns planted on the hill above. It was the first real day of spring. At night they danced again, but broke it off when rumors spread that the militia were preparing to attack.

The next morning, April 20, it happened.

Three signal bombs burst over the tent colony. John Reed tells what took place next:

Suddenly, without warning, both machine guns pounded stab-stab-stab full on the tents.

It was premeditated and merciless. Militiamen have told me that their orders were to destroy the tent colony and everything living in it. The three bombs were a signal to the mine-guards and Baldwin-Felts detectives and strike-breakers in the neighboring mines; and they came swarming down out of the hills fully armed—four hundred of them.

Suddenly the terrible storm of lead from the machine guns ripped their coverings to pieces, and the most awful panic followed. Some of the women and children streamed out over the plain, to get away from the tent colony. They were shot at as they ran. Others with the unarmed men took refuge in the arroyo to the north. Mrs. Fyler led a group of women and children, under fire, to the deep well at the railroad pump house, down which they climbed on ladders. Others still crept into the bullet proof cellars they had dug for themselves under their tents.

The fighting men, appalled at what was happening, started for the tent colony; but they were driven back by a hail of bullets. And now the mine-guards began to get into action, shooting explosive bullets, which burst with the report of a six-shooter all through the tents. The machine guns never let up. Tikas [Louis Tikas, popular leader of the Greek miners] had started off with the Greeks; but he ran back in a desperate attempt to save some of those who remained; and stayed in the tent colony all day. He and Mrs. Jolly, the wife of an American striker, and Bernardo, leader of the Italians, and Domeniski, leader of the Slavs, carried water and food and bandages to those imprisoned in the cellars. There was no one shooting from the tent colony. Not a man there had a gun. Tikas thought that the explosive bullets were the sound of shots being fired from the tents, and ran round like a crazy man to tell the fool to stop. It was an hour before he discovered what really made the noise.

Mrs. Jolly put on a white dress; and Tikas and Domeniski made big red crosses and pinned them on her breast and arms. The militia used them as targets. Her dress was riddled in a dozen places, and the heel of her shoe shot off. So fierce was the fire wherever she went that the people had to beg her to keep away from them. Undaunted, she and the three men made sandwiches and drew water to carry to the women and children.

Early that morning an armored train was made up in Trinidad, and 126 militiamen of Troop A got on board. But the trainmen refused to take them; and it was not until three o'clock in the afternoon that they finally found a crew to man the train. They got to Ludlow about four o'clock, and added their two machine guns to the terrible fire poured unceasingly into the tent colony. One detachment slowly drove the strikers out of their position at the arroyo, and another attempted in vain to dislodge those in the railroad. Lieutenant Linderfelt, in command of eight militiamen firing from the windows of the railroad station, ordered them to "shoot every God damned thing that moves!" Captain Carson came up to Major Hamrock and reminded him respectfully that they had only a few hours of daylight left to burn the tent colony. "Burn them out! Smoke them out!" yelled the officers. And their men poured death into the tents in a fury of blood lust.

It was growing dark. The militia closed in around the tent colony. At about 7:30, a militiaman with a bucket of kerosene and a broom ran up to the first tent, wet it thoroughly, and touched a match to it. The flame roared up, illuminating the whole countryside. Other soldiers fell upon the other tents; and in a minute the whole northwest corner of the colony was aflame. A freight train came along just then with orders to stop on a siding near the pump house; and the women and children in the well took advantage of the protection of the train to creep out along the right-of-way fence to the protection of the arroyo, screaming and crying. A dozen militiamen jumped to the engineer's cab and thrust guns in his face yelling to him to move on or they would shoot him. He obeyed; and in the flickering light of the burning tents the militia shot at the refugees again and again. At the first leap of the flames the astounded strikers ceased firing; but the militia did not. They poured among the tents, shouting with the fury of destruction, smashing open trunks and looting.

When the fire started Mrs. Jolly went from tent to tent, pulling the women and children out of the cellars and herding them before her out on the plain. She remembered all of a sudden that Mrs. Petrucci and her three children were in the cellar under her tent, and started back to get them out. "No," said Tikas, "you go ahead with that bunch. I'll go back after the Petruccis." And he started toward the flames.

There the militia captured him. He tried to explain his errand; but they were drunk with blood lust and would not listen to him. Lieutenant Linderfelt broke the stock of his rifle over the Greek's head, laying it open to the bone. Fifty men got a rope and threw it over a telegraph wire to hang him. But Linderfelt cynically handed him over to two militiamen, and told them they were responsible for his life. Five minutes later Louis Tikas fell dead with three bullets in his back; and out of Mrs. Petrucci's cellar were afterward taken the charred bodies of thirteen women and children.

Fyler, too, they captured and murdered, shooting him fifty-four times. Above the noise of the flames and the shouting came the screaming of women and children, burning to death under the floors of their tents. Some were pulled out by the soldiers, beaten and kicked and arrested. Others were allowed to die without any effort being made to save them. An American striker named Snyder crouched dully in his tent beside the body of his eleven-year-old son, the back of whose head had been blown off by an explosive bullet. One militiaman came into the tent, soaked it with kerosene and set it on fire, hitting Snyder over the head with his rifle and telling him to beat it. Snyder pointed to the body of his boy; and the soldier dragged it outside by the collar, threw it on the ground, and said: "Here! Carry the damned thing yourself!"

Reed went over to Ludlow to see what it looked like after the massacre:

The tent colony, or where the tent colony had been, was a great square of ghastly ruins. Stoves, pots and pans still full of food that had been cooking that terrible morning, baby carriages, piles of half-burned clothes, children's toys all riddled with bullets, the scorched mouths of the tent cellars, and the children's toys that we found at the bottom of the "death hole"—this was all that remained of the entire worldly possessions of 1,200 poor people.

Inquiring into the Colorado strike, the House Committee on Mines and Mining questioned John D. Rockefeller Jr.:

QUESTION: *You are willing to let these killings take place rather than to go there and do something to settle conditions?*

ANSWER: *There is just one thing that can be done to settle this strike, and that is to unionize the camps, and our interest in labor is so profound and we believe so sincerely that that interest demands that the camps be open camps, that we expect to stand by the officers at any cost . . .*

QUESTION: *And you will do that if that costs all your property and kills all your employees?*

ANSWER: *It is a great principle.*

For that principle of no union at any cost, the miners paid with 33 dead that day at Ludlow and over 100 wounded.

News of the Ludlow massacre spread like wildfire. That same night men (not only strikers) with all the guns they could lay their hands on started for Ludlow. For 10 days the region was a battlefield over which a workers' army clashed with government and company forces. The governor appealed to Washington for federal troops to put down "open insurrection against the State." With their arrival, Colorado's civil war ended.

The strike went on through the summer and fall, but every attempt to get the company to deal with the union failed. After 15 months of hunger, blood and death, Rockefeller forced the workers to accept a company union.

Ludlow horrified the nation. The U.S. Commission sent investigators to the scene and took evidence from all sides.

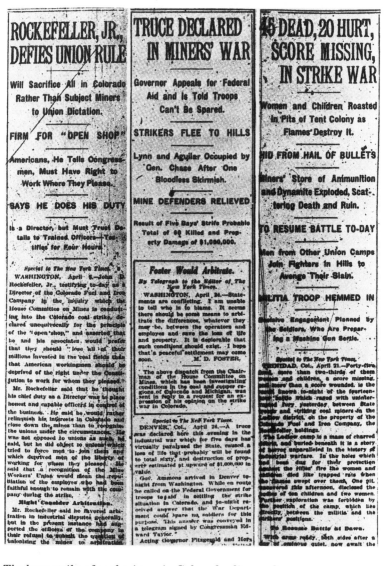

The long strike of coal miners in Colorado climaxed in 1914 in what became known as the Ludlow Massacre. These dispatches to the New York Times *drew national attention to the tragedy.* (Courtesy New York Public Library)

Then it held hearings in the East and summoned John D. Rockefeller Jr. to testify. He pleaded ignorance of conditions in his Colorado mines and insisted he was not opposed to labor unions. But Commission researchers had unearthed a pile of letters between Rockefeller and the mine managers. At the next session they confronted Rockefeller with the proof that, in the Commission's words, "he followed, step by step, the struggle of his executive officials to retain arbitrary power, and to prevent the installation of machinery for collective bargaining, by which abuses might automatically be corrected, and he supported and encouraged this struggle in every letter he wrote to his agents."

Rockefeller said that the hearings had given him a new conception of "the kinship of humanity." But the Colorado Fuel & Iron Company kept its company union, and not until 1933 did it recognize the United Mine Workers.

18

CONCLUSION

The Colorado mine strike and Ludlow showed what workers were up against when they tried to organize. But in case anyone thought that was exceptional, the U.S. Commission on Industrial Relations added many other examples to the record.

It went into the field and took evidence about a great number of strikes in every part of the country—the Los Angeles printers strike, the Paterson silk strike, the Bethlehem Steel strike, the New York City garment workers strike, strikes by lumbermen, rubber workers, transit workers, brewery workers, railroad workers, metal workers.

"Freedom does not exist either politically, industrially or socially," for workers who want to organize or go on strike, the Commission reported:

> Almost without exception the employees of large corporations are unorganized, as a result of the active and aggressive "non-union" policy of the corporation managements. Our Rockefellers, Morgans, Fricks, Vanderbilts and Astors can do no industrial wrong because all effective action and direct responsibility is shifted from them to executive officials.

But the Commission would not accept such attempts to mask responsibility. Its hearings gave labor a chance to tell its own story in its own way. And for the first time in

American history, the employers—like Rockefeller—were made to defend themselves before the public.

In part, the Commission documented for Americans what they already knew—that the America of the early 1900s was an age of industrial violence. The swift growth of industry and the enormous power of the corporations had got beyond the country's control. Social reformers feared that as the 20th century advanced, society would be torn to pieces unless a way was found to reshape it.

The Progressive movement in city after city, as early as the 1890s, had already improved local conditions and government. And since cities were under the dominance of state government, the reformers had to work for changes in statewide laws, too. One by one the states, under this pressure, began to pass laws for the benefit of industrial workers.

Legislation on child labor is a good example of what an awakened public conscience tried to do. Around 1900 the children stood alone, the law blind to their exploitation. In 1904 a National Child Labor Committee was formed, and soon two out of three states had child labor laws. Unfortunately, the laws did not as a rule cover farm work or domestic service, nor were they very effective. Employer opposition remained bitter. A federal law was passed in 1916 to cover all children who had any part in making products that passed from one state to another. But two years later the Supreme Court declared it unconstitutional. A year later another federal attempt was made, and again the court struck it down. (Not until 1938 would a federal law regulating child labor go through—as part of the Fair Labor Standards Act—which the court would let stand.)

The hours women worked were limited by many states during this period. Safety regulations were widely adopted to reduce the danger of industrial accidents; factory inspection systems were devised; workers compensation laws were passed; and there were even federal attempts to regulate monopoly.

The fighting mood of that era won the people several gains and made living a little easier. Even as the reforms were being passed, however, the great gap between rich and poor was growing ever wider. Reform government invariably gave way again to corrupt political machines. "The masters of the government of the United States," Woodrow Wilson could still say in 1913, "are the combined capitalists and manufacturers of the United States."

Yet the president was hopeful this might not always be. He knew there was a great power for progress whose energy had never yet been fully tapped. "A nation is as great, and only as great, as her rank and file," he said.

Again and again in those 50 years between the Civil War and the First World War, the rank and file of labor had risen hopefully to demand a chance in the fight for life. They built the craft form of organization and then, when the great industrial empires developed, went on to create the industrial union to embrace the millions working in the basic industries. The history of their struggles, as set down here in the documents, shows how fiercely they had to fight for every gain they made. The refusal of the titans of industry to grant them the most elementary democratic rights—free speech, free press, free assembly—led time and again to violence and death. Homestead, Pullman, Lawrence, Ludlow: The names are labor's honor roll, for there and in countless other places working men and women proved they would not let themselves be treated as so much horsepower to do the nation's work. Their sweat and blood, their faith and pain, had made America great. They wanted an end to ignorance and poverty and cruelty. They wanted to shape a future of fellowship and freedom.

The struggle for bread—and roses, too—still goes on. Another 75 years and more have passed since the period that ends this book, and yet in an affluent America, vast numbers of workers are still unorganized. And tens of millions are still living at levels below human decency. They know hunger; they lack adequate housing, and education, and medical care; they are often denied their human rights. They are America's poor, the unskilled and the migrant workers, the aged, the minorities, the homeless, the rejects of society.

The story has no end, of course. The struggle for ever more freedom and for a fuller measure of human dignity is never over.

A SHORT DICTIONARY
OF LABOR TERMS

apprentice a person trained for a skilled trade by experience on the job, combined with instruction by a skilled worker. Completion of apprenticeship leads to journeyman status.

arbitration the method of settling disagreements between employers and workers by having an impartial person or committee decide them.

blacklist a secret list of names of union members and organizers developed and exchanged by employers and employers' associations to keep such "undesirable" or "troublesome" people from getting jobs. It was declared an unfair labor practice by federal law in 1935.

boycott the organized refusal to buy, and to get others to refuse to buy, products or services produced in a nonunion plant or by an employer accused of unfair labor practices. The aim is to win concessions from the employer. The term comes from an Irish landlord named Boycott, whose tenant farmers used this weapon against him.

brotherhood the name used by some of the older unions, especially the railroad unions, which were started as fraternal or benefit organizations stressing the brotherhood of man.

check weighman   the man who weighs or measures the coal produced by each miner being paid on a tonnage basis. The aim is to make sure the miner is not cheated.

closed shop   a place of work that has made an agreement with a union not to hire anyone who is not a member of the union or who does not keep in good standing with the union. (Closed shops were declared illegal by federal law in 1947.)

collective bargaining   the negotiation between employer and union to reach an agreement on the terms and conditions of employment for a definite period. It was established as a legal right in the 1930s.

company store   a retail store owned and run by a company whose main business is something else. The company store was for the use of the workers and their families. Often higher prices were charged and wages paid in scrip usable only in the company store, forcing the workers to shop there. Few company stores of this kind remain.

company town   a place lived in solely or chiefly by the workers of a single company, which owns all or most of the property and homes and in effect runs the local government. These were often set up by the employer to keep unions out or to avoid higher taxes.

company union   a labor organization set up by and often run by employers to prevent regular unions from coming in, and to control labor to their own advantage. It is now outlawed as an unfair labor practice.

craft union   a labor organization limiting membership to persons with some specific skill, such as electricians or plumbers. Usually the craft union controls apprenticeship training. They are "horizontal" in form. (See INDUSTRIAL UNION.)

depression   a falloff in general business activity resulting in widespread and long-lasting unemployment. In some industries depressions occur more or less regularly on a seasonal basis, perhaps once or twice a year.

discrimination   unfair treatment of a particular group of workers or an individual worker for reasons of race, religion, national origin, age, sex or union membership. It has nothing to do with a worker's ability to perform the job, and can affect hiring, layoffs, wages and promotions. Discrimination can also be practiced by a union against workers, as when a union refuses to admit blacks to membership or to apprentice training programs.

general strike   a widespread strike in which workers throughout a city or throughout the country take part, regardless of industry or union.

homework   the making of products in private homes or tenements from material supplied by an employer. The worker is paid by the hour or by the piece. It usually meant low wages and long hours and often involved whole families.

industrial union   a labor organization that takes in all or most of the occupations, whether skilled or unskilled, within an entire industry. Sometimes called *vertical* organization, as opposed to the *horizontal* organization of craft unions.

injunction   an order from a judge commanding an individual or a union not to do certain things, such as picketing, or striking or boycotting. Refusal to obey means a legal penalty, such as a fine or jail sentence, or both.

journeyman   a worker in a skilled trade who has served an apprenticeship to qualify for such work.

lockout   the shutting down of a plant by employers to force workers to accept their terms. Sometimes the workers convert the lockout into a strike.

mudsill   a person of the lowest level of society. A term common in the South, often used with contempt.

open shop   in theory, a plant where both union and nonunion members are hired. Actually, however, employers who campaigned for the "open shop" intended to keep out all union members. "Open shop" soon came to mean "closed to union members."

picketing   the placing by a labor organization of one or more members, usually carrying signs, at the entrance to a shop during a labor dispute. The purpose is to let the public and the workers know that there is a dispute, to persuade workers to join or help carry on the strike or boycott and to keep people from entering or working in the shop.

piecework   the form of payment to a worker based upon a fixed sum for each article produced or worked on. Earnings therefore go up or down according to output.

sabotage   the act of stopping or interfering with production in order to pressure the employer. It is a direct action method, which used to range from peaceful limiting of output to the destruction of machines and materials. In recent times it usually means the latter. *Soldiering* or *slowdown* are the terms for the deliberate and peaceful slowing down of effort.

scab   a worker who continues to work during a strike. It can also mean one who takes a job in a nonunion shop or under nonunion conditions when a union is trying to organize the industry.

scrip   a certificate given out by an employer in place of cash wages. Usually it is accepted only at a company store.

speedup   an increase in the worker's effort forced by the employer without an accompanying increase in pay. It can be done by speeding up the machine's rate, by demanding more units of production from the worker or by asking the worker to tend more machines.

spy   a person hired by an employer, either directly or through a private detective agency, to keep a watch on union members and their activities. The information is desired by the employer to help break up a union. Sometimes spies become union members and do their work from inside. Or they may work from outside, associating with workers in the neighborhood or town.

strike   the stopping of work by a group of workers to pressure the employer into settling a grievance or granting changes in pay or working conditions.

strikebreakers   persons hired by employers or their agents to fill the jobs of workers on strike. Sometimes they are hired only for the limited period of the strike. At other times the intention is to keep them on as permanent workers. The term also refers to spies and scabs or to toughs hired to break up a strike by violence.

syndicalism   a term for trade unionism originally used in France. In the United States it came to mean the revolutionary idea that syndicates or unions should take over industries and run them for the benefit of the workers and of society. The Industrial Workers of the World, organized in the early 1900s, were syndicalists in this sense.

timework   the form of paying a worker based upon a fixed sum for each hour or each day.

union shop   an agreement between union and employer that requires all workers to join the union immediately upon being hired or within a specific period afterwards and to remain members.

wages   the regular payment for work done under normal conditions, that is, not including overtime or holiday work.

yellow-dog contract   the term workers coined for the pledge employers once forced their workers to sign in order to get a job. The worker promised not to join a union.

BIBLIOGRAPHY

Included here are many of the sources used in the preparation of this book. Other titles are offered as suggestions for further reading and research. All are arranged under general subject headings, where there is considerable overlap. Don't conclude your research on a particular subject before checking other, similar areas.

Many of these titles are out of print, but in most cases you should have no problem locating them with the assistance of your librarian.

GENERAL LABOR HISTORY
The social, political and economic background against which labor developed is detailed in Joseph Rayback's *A History of American Labor*, New York, Free Press, 1966. Earlier studies include the classic John R. Commons, *History of Labor in the United States*, 4 vols. (New York: Augustus Kelley, 1966); Norman Ware's *The Labor Movement in the United States 1860–1895* (reprint Magnolia, Mass.: Peter Smith, 1959); and Mary R. Beard's *The American Labor Movement* (Philadelphia: Ayer, 1969). A widely used textbook is *Labor in America*, Foster R. Dulles and Melvyn Dubofsky, eds., 4th rev. ed. (Arlington Heights, Ill.: Harlan Davidson, 1984). There are several recent works by scholars that are challenging and highly readable: David Brody, *Workers in Industrial America: Essays*

on the 20th Century Struggle (New York: Oxford University Press, 1981); David Montgomery, The Fall of the House of Labor: The Workplace, the State, and American Labor Activism (New York: Cambridge University Press, 1987); and Richard B. Morris, ed., A History of the American Worker (Princeton, N.J.: Princeton University Press, 1983). The testimony of workers and employers, re-creating the conditions that led millions to organize in unions, is contained in Leon Litwack's American Labor Movement (New York: Prentice Hall, 1962). A more recent collection of documents is The Labor History Reader, Daniel Leab, ed. (Champaign: University of Illinois Press, 1985). Workers Speak: Self-Portraits 1902–1906 (Philadelphia: Ayer, 1971) brings the reader close to the life of the individual worker.

IMMIGRANT WORKERS

Scholars give considerable attention to the part played by immigrants in the labor movement. One overall view is Dirk Hoeder, American Labor and Immigration History, 1877–1920: Recent European Research (Champaign: University of Illinois Press, 1983). Examples of focus on specific ethnic groups are Edwin Fenton, Immigrants and Unions: A Case Study of Italians and American Labor (Philadelphia: Ayer, 1975); Melech Epstein, Jewish Labor in the U.S.A., 1882–1952 (Hoboken, N.J.: Ktav, 1969); and Robert Parmet, Labor and Immigration in Industrial America (Melbourne, Fla.: Krieger, 1987).

WOMEN WORKERS

Recovering the forgotten or obscured role of women workers in this era, many feminist scholars are producing studies both general and specialized. Rosalyn Baxandall, in America's Working Women: A Documentary History— 1600 to the Present (New York: Random House, 1976), begins her story in 1600 and continues it to the 1970s. James J. Keneally, Women and American Trade Unions, 2nd ed. (St. Louis: Eden, 1981), is another general history. Studies that provide social as well as industrial history include Kathy Preiss, Cheap Amusements: Working Women & Leisure in Turn-of-the-Century New York (Philadelphia: Temple University Press, 1985); and Diane Van Raaphorst, *Union Maids Not Wanted: Organizing Domestic Workers 1870–1940* (New York: Praeger, 1988). Mary E. (Mother) Jones, one of the most prominent labor organizers of this time, has had three books devoted to her life and work: Dale Fetherling's *Mother Jones, the Miner's Angel: A Portrait* (Carbondale: Southern Illinois University Press, 1974); *Mother Jones Speaks: Her Collected Writings and Speeches*, edited by Philip Foner, Anchor Foundation, 1983; and *The Correspondence of Mother Jones*, Edward Steel, ed. (Pittsburgh: University of Pittsburgh Press, 1985).

BIOGRAPHIES OF LABOR LEADERS

For brief sketches of leader's lives, there are Gary M. Fink's *Biographical Dictionary of American Labor* (Westport, Conn.: Greenwood Press, 1984); and Joyce Bellamy and John Saville, eds., *Dictionary of Labour Biography*, 8 vols. (New York: Augustus Kelley, 1972–1987). Terence V. Powderly tells his own story of the Knights of Labor in *Thirty Years of Life and Labor*, rev. ed. (New York: Augustus Kelley, 1967). Ray Ginger's *The Bending Cross*, 1949 (reissued as *Eugene V. Debs: A Biography* [New York: Macmillan, 1962]) is a life of Eugene V. Debs. William D. Haywood's autobiography is called *Bill Haywood's Book* (Westport, Conn.: Greenwood Press, 1983). A large-scale biography of Haywood is Melvyn Dubofsky's *"Big Bill" Haywood* (New York: St. Martin's Press, 1987). Samuel Gompers' autobiography is *Seventy Years of Life and Labor* (New York: Augustus Kelley, 1967).

GREAT STRIKES

Detailed accounts of several of the major strikes occurring in 1865–1915 can be found in several books. Samuel Yellen's *American Labor Struggles*, reprint, Anchor Foundation, 1974, embraces many of them, and *American Violence, a Documentary History* (New York: Random House, 1971), edited by Richard Hofstadter and Michael Wallace, includes documents describing a number of them under the heading "Economic Violence," Part II. Titles devoted to single events are: Henry David, *History of the*

Haymarket Affair (New York: Russell & Russell, 1958); Lindsey Almont, *The Pullman Strike* (Chicago: University of Chicago Press, 1964); Robert Bruce, *1877: Year of Violence*, reprint (Chicago: Ivan Dee, 1989), which covers the great railroad strike of that year; Zeese Papanikolas, *Buried Unsung: Louis Tikas and the Ludlow Massacre* (Salt Lake City: Books On Demand, 1990); and William Cahn's *Lawrence 1912: The Bread and Roses Strike* (New York: Pilgrim, 1980).

CHILD LABOR
Reporters and photographers who investigated the conditions of children in the mines, mills and fields produced books designed to rally support for legislation preventing harm to young workers. These included Jacob Riis's *Children of the Poor*, reprint (Philadelphia: Ayer, 1971), and his *Children of the Tenements*, New York, originally printed in 1903 but since reprinted by Irvington, New York; his *How the Other Half Lives: Studies Among the Tenements of New York*, reprint (Magnolia, Mass.: Peter Smith, 1988) also contains much on children. The great documentary photographer of that era, Lewis Hine, produced *Photographs of Child Labor in the New South*, Mississippi, reprint, 1986. The poet, Edwin Markham, who wrote "Man With the Hoe," investigated child labor and published *Children in Bondage*, reprint (Philadelphia: Ayer, 1969). Finally, a passionate protest is voiced in *The Bitter Cry of the Children*, reprint (New York: Irvington, 1972) by John Spargo.

THE AFRICAN AMERICAN WORKER
Excellent documents are provided by Philip S. Foner and Ronald C. Lewis, eds., *The Black Worker: A documentary History from Colonial Times to the Present* (Philadelphia: Temple University Press, 1984). A narrative history by Foner is *Organized Labor and the Black Worker* (New York: International Publishers, 1982).

THE MUCKRAKERS
Some of the most colorful and penetrating writing of the era has been collected in several anthologies: Harvey

Swados, *Years of Conscience: The Muckrakers*, World, 1962; Arthur and Lila Weinberg, *The Muckrakers* (New York: Putnam, 1964); and Richard Hofstadter, *The Progressive Movement 1900–1915* (New York: Simon & Schuster, 1986). Robert Hunter produced a pioneering study of the poor of that era in *Poverty*, reprint (New York: Irvington, 1972); and Ray Stannard Baker described black life in *Following the Color Line*, reprint (Williamstown, Mass.: Corner House, 1973). A study of that era's investigating journalism is in David M. Chalmer's *The Social and Political Ideas of the Muckrakers* (Philadelphia: Ayer, 1964).

ABOUT INDUSTRIES, OCCUPATIONS AND COMMUNITIES

Social historians are giving us new ideas about labor history, cutting across the divisions of industrial, urban and immigrant history. A prime example of this creative approach is *Work, Culture and Society in Industrializing America: Essays in America's Working Class and Social History* (New York: Random House, 1977) by Herbert G. Gutman. In *Men, Women, and Work: Class, Gender and Protest in the New England Shoe Industry 1780–1907* (Chicago: University of Illinois Press, 1988), Mary H. Blewett examines our understanding of an industry and a community. S. J. Kleinberg, in *The Shadow of the Mills* (Pittsburgh: University of Pittsburgh Press, 1989), describes working-class families in Pittsburgh between 1870 and 1907. Priscilla Long, in *Where the Sun Never Shines* (New York: Paragon, 1989), provides an in-depth account of the bloody coal history in the United States until 1920. Mark Wyman takes us to the other side of the continent in his *Hard Rock Epic: Western Miners and the Industrial Revolution, 1860–1910* (Berkeley: University of California Press, 1989).

In *Homestead: The Households of a Milltown* (Pittsburgh: University of Pittsburgh Press, 1974), Margaret Byington gets behind the Homestead steel strike and shows how the working people lived in a company town. Tamara K. Hareven takes a similar approach in *Amoskeag: Life and Work in an American Factory-City* (New York: Pantheon, 1980); and David G. McCullough, in *The Johnstown Flood* (New York: Simon & Schuster, 1987), reveals working-class life in Pennsylvania during this period.

Novels are often invaluable for an intimate depiction of life, and in Upton Sinclair's classic expose, *The Jungle* (Champaign: University of Illinois Press, 1988), we see the terrible working and living conditions of the immigrants who labored in Chicago's meat packing industry at the turn of the century.

MUSIC AND FILM

American Labor Songs of the 19th Century (Champaign: University of Illinois Press, 1975), edited by Philip S. Foner, and *The Ballad of America: The History of the United States in Song and Story* (Carbondale: Southern Illinois University Press, 1983), edited by John Anthony Scott, provide the words and music of many songs of the 1865–1915 era. See also Pete Seeger and Bob Reiser, *Carry It On: A History in Song and Picture of the Working Men and Women of America* (New York: Simon and Schuster, 1985). *The Bread and Roses Strike: Lawrence, 1912* is a 20-minute film documentary written by Milton Meltzer and produced by New York Local Union 1199.

INDEX

A

Accidents, in industry, 20, 25, 96, 116, 137, 151
Addams, Jane, 112
African-Americans: excluded from railway union, 92; discriminated against by white workers, 54-56; form national union, 56; and National Labor Union, 54-56
Altgeld, John Peter, 83-86, 90
Amalgamated Association of Iron and Steel Workers, 94-102
American Federation of Labor, 87-90, 95, 117, 118, 124
American Railway Union, 92-93; in Pullman strike, 106-11
Anarchists, 76-83
Arbitration, 70, 107
Armour, Philip, 36
Atkinson, Henry A., 141

B

Baker, Ray Stannard, 120-27, 130
Baldwin-Felts detectives, 141, 143
Beecher, Henry Ward, 42, 62
Bellamy, Edward, 113
Blacklisting, 70, 101
Borah, William T., 129
Boycotts, 70, 107-10

"Bread—and Roses" poem, 132-33
Bribery, 39, 42
Bryan, William Jennings, 115
Byington, Margaret, 95

C

Candler, Asa G., 18
Carnegie, Andrew, 36, 95, 97, 100, 101
Carnegie Steel Corporation, 66, 94-102
Child labor, 18-25; in candy factory, 21; in coal mines, 19-21; making artificial flowers, 21; in textile mills, 18, 24, 121
Chinese workers, 68
Cigar makers, 7-9, 28
Civil War, 1, 3, 12, 36, 37, 39, 94, 114, 152
Cleveland, Grover, 89, 108, 112, 114
Coal miners, 135-49
Colorado Fuel and Iron Company, 133, 141
Colored Caulkers' Trades Union Society, 55
Company towns, 15, 103-05, 133
Convict labor, 71
Conwell, Russell H., 41, 43
Cooke, Jay, 42, 48

Corruption: by mine owners, 137; in politics, 38, 39, 42, 62, 124; of the press, 42; on railroad construction, 38

Cost of living, 10, 73, 122, 130

Craft unions, 88-89

Credit Mobilier scandal, 39

D

Debs, Eugene Victor; builds craft union, 90; leads Pullman strike, 106-11; organizes industrial union, 92-93; as Socialist candidate for president, 117

Democratic Party, 115

democratic rights, 152

Depressions: causes of, 44-45; of 1870s, 44-49, 77; of 1883, 70; of 1893, 106

Douglass, Frederick, 55

Douglass, Lewis, 55

Duke, James B., 37

E

Ebert, Justus, 119

Eight-hour movement, 51-52, 56

Ettor, Joseph, 125, 126, 130

F

Fair Labor Standards Act, 151

Field, Marshall, 36

Fielden, Samuel, 78

Fisk, Jim, 36

Fitch, John, 98, 133

Flynn, Elizabeth Gurley, 125, 128-29

Frick, Henry Clay, 97-98, 101

G

Garfield, James A., 39

Garland, Hamlin, 96

Garment workers, 16-17, 28-31

General Managers Association, 107, 109

George, Henry, 36, 113

Gilded Age, 38

Giovannitti, Arturo, 125, 126, 130, 134

Gompers, Samuel, 7-9, 28, 87, 95, 110, 117

Gould, Jay, 36, 37-38, 71

H

Hayes, Rutherford B., 58-60

Haymarket bombing, 76-78, 115

Haywood, William D., 125, 126

Health: of child labor, 18-25; of tenement dwellers, 26-33; of textile workers, 123; of women workers, 12-17

Hill, James J., 92-93

"home work" system, 28-30

Homeless, 45

Homestead strike, 94-102, 152

Hours of work: 11, 12, 18, 21; of child labor, 18-25; and eight-hour movement, 51-52, 74; limited by states, 151; in steel mills, 95; of women, 12-17; in 1880s, 73; in 1910, 116

Hours of work: 11, 12, 18, 21; of child labor, 18-25; and eight-hour movement, 51-52, 74; limited by states, 151; in steel mills, 95; of women, 12-17; in 1880s, 73; in 1910, 116

Housing, 26-28, 104, 136

Howells, William Dean, 82, 129

Hull House, 112

Hunger, 45

Hunter, Robert, 21, 33, 115

Huntington, Collis P., 42

I

Immigrants: in Homestead steel strike, 94-102; imported by industry, 66; in Lawrence textile strike, 119-33; in Ludlow mine strike, 138; organized by IWW, 121-22, 125; prejudice against, 68-70; used as strikebreakers, 67

Industrial revolution, 1-3

Industrial Workers of the World (IWW), 118, 124-32

Injunctions, 109-11

International Typographical
Union, 55
International Workingmen's As-
sociation, 53

K
Knight of Labor, 68-74, 87

L
Labor songs, 74-75, 76, 102, 127,
132-33, 143
Labor spies, 70
Landlords, 28
Lawrence, Mass., strike, 119-33,
134, 152
Lindsey, Almont, 104
Lindsey, Ben, 129
Lloyd, Henry Demarest, 82
Ludlow, Colo. strike, 134-49
Ludlow massacre, 144-47, 152

M
McGowan, Kenneth, 130
Machinist, on downgrading skill,
4-5
Marx, Karl, 53
Mechanization, 4-9, 101
Mellon, Thomas, 36
Miller, Samuel F., 63
Monopoly, 37
Morgan, J.P., 36, 37, 41
Muckrakers, 115-16
Myers, Isaac, 56

N
National Child Labor Committee,
151
National Colored Labor Union, 56
National Guard, used against
strikers, 100, 143
National Labor Union, 50-56

O
Olney, Richard, 108
Oppenheim, James, 132

P
Paris Commune, 61

Parsons, Albert, 76-83
Parsons, Lucy, 77, 83
Pinkerton detectives, in Home-
stead strike, 94-102
Populist Party, 114-15
Poverty: in 1870s, 44-49; in 1890,
35-36
Powderly, Terence, 70, 71
Printers, 13
Progressive movement, 115-17,
151
Pullman, George W., 103-11, 112
Pullman strike, 103-11, 112, 152

R
Race prejudice, 54-55, 92
Railroad workers: in Pullman
strike, 103-11; in strike of 1877,
57-65
Railroads, 1-2
Rauschenbusch, Walter, 113
Red scares, 61, 80, 126
Reed, John, 136, 138, 142, 144
Reform movement, 112-18
Religion, 37
Rhodes, James Ford, 61
Riis, Jacob, 26-28, 30
Rockefeller, John D., 36, 37, 43,
133, 140
Rockefeller, John D. Jr., 133, 140,
147-49, 151
Roosevelt, Theodore, 116
Robber barons, 39

S
Scabs, *see* strikebreaking
Sherman Anti-Trust Act, 108
Shoemakers, 6-7
Slums, *see* Housing
Social gospel, 113
Socialist Party, 117
Soup kitchens, 46
Spargo, John, 19
Speculative fever, 37, 44
Spies, August, 77-83
Steel workers, 5
Steward, Ira, 51
Stephens, Uriah, 68

Strasser, Adolph, 87
Strikebreaking, 46, 55, 64, 70, 77, 94, 100, 143
Strikes, 50, 150; at Homestead, 94-102 115; at Ludlow, 134-39; at Pullman, 106-11, 112; on railroads in 1877, 57-65, 115; for shorter hours, 76
Sweatshops, 28-33
Swinton, John, 46, 66, 74
Sylvis, William H., 53-56

T
Taft, William Howard, 130
Taft, Mrs. William Howard, 129
Tenements, *see* Housing
Textile workers: of Holyoke, Mass., 9-10; of Lawrence, Mass., 119-33; of Lowell, Mass., 1; of Manchester, N.H., 22-23; of Paterson, N.J., 2-3, 18; of South Carolina, 13-14, 23-24
Tikas, Louis, 144-46
Trumbull, Lyman, 82
Trusts, 37-41, 89
Twain, Mark, 36, 43, 44

U
Unemployed demonstration, 47-49
Unemployment, in depression of 1870s, 44-49
Unions, 50-56, 150-52; before Civil War, 51; and black labor, 54; organized by craft, 87-90; and eight-hour day, 51-52; organized by industry, 92-93; and strikes, 57-65, 92-93, 94-102,

103-11; and women workers, 53-54
United Mine Workers, 139
U.S. Commission on Industrial Relations, 136, 140, 142, 147-49, 150
U.S. Labor Bureau, 139
U.S. Supreme Court, 83, 110, 151

V
Van Vorst, Marie, 13, 23

W
Wages, 6, 9-10, 11, 12-13, 15, 16, 19; of children, 18-25; in coal mines, 136; as system of control, 134; cut in depressions, 49, 57-58; cut on railroads, 57-65; at Pullman, 105-06; raised by AF of L, 89; in steel mills, 95; in sweatshops, 30-31; in textile mills, 121; in 1910, 116
Walker, Edwin, 108
Warner, John D., 28
Wealthy: contrasted with poor, 116-17, 152; and gospel of success, 41-42; increase in millionaires, 35; as philanthropists, 123; style of living, 34-37; under attack, 39-41
Weaver, James B., 39
Welborn, J.F., 138, 139
Whitman, Walt, 43
Whitney, Eli, 2
Wilson, Woodrow, 116, 152
Women workers, 6, 12-17; in 1900, 17; in textile mills, 121
World War I, 152
Wright, Carroll D., 71

MILTON MELTZER, distinguished historian and biographer, is the author of more than 80 books for young people and adults. Born in Worcester, Massachusetts and educated at Columbia University, he worked for the WPA Federal Theatre Project and then served in the Air Force in World War II. He has also written for newspapers, magazines, radio, television and films.

Among the many honors for his books are five nominations for the National Book Award, as well as the Christopher, Edison, Jane Addams, Carter G. Woodson, Jefferson Cup, Washington Book Guild, Olive Branch and Golden Kite awards. Many of his titles have been named ALA Notable Children's Books, and have been included in Notable Children's Trade Books in the Field of Social Studies. His first book, *A Pictorial History of Black Americans*, written with Langston Hughes and in print for 35 years, has recently been adapted by Scholastic as a textbook retitled *African American History*.

Mr. Meltzer is a member of the Authors Guild. He lives with his wife in New York City. They have two daughters and a grandson.